Thirty Days in God's Presence

Thirty Days
in
God's Presence

DAVID L. MATHEWSON
& JENNIFER J. FITZGERALD

Foreword by Peter Young

WIPF & STOCK · Eugene, Oregon

THIRTY DAYS IN GOD'S PRESENCE

Copyright © 2024 David L. Mathewson and Jennifer J. Fitzgerald. All rights reserved. Except for brief quotations in critical publications or reviews, no part of this book may be reproduced in any manner without prior written permission from the publisher. Write: Permissions, Wipf and Stock Publishers, 199 W. 8th Ave., Suite 3, Eugene, OR 97401.

Wipf & Stock
An Imprint of Wipf and Stock Publishers
199 W. 8th Ave., Suite 3
Eugene, OR 97401

www.wipfandstock.com

PAPERBACK ISBN: 979-8-3852-1067-1
HARDCOVER ISBN: 979-8-3852-1068-8
EBOOK ISBN: 979-8-3852-1069-5

VERSION NUMBER 052224

Contents

Foreword by Peter Young | vii
Introduction | xi

Day 1: It Begins with Delight | 1

Day 2: Entering in through the Tabernacle | 5

Day 3: Becoming a Fragrant Incense | 11

Day 4: Resting in God's Presence | 15

Day 5: Priests in God's Service | 20

Day 6: God's Name and God's Dwelling | 24

Day 7: A Home for God's Presence | 28

Day 8: Who Can Approach God's Presence? | 33

Day 9: Climbing the Lord's Holy Hill | 37

Day 10: Gazing on the Lord's Beauty | 42

Day 11: Desiring God | 46

Day 12: Ascending into God's Presence | 51

Day 13: Ascending into God's Presence | 56

Day 14: Intimacy with God | 60

Day 15: A Glimpse of God's Holiness | 66

Day 16: Vision of a Future Temple | 70

Day 17: The Life-Giving Water of God's Presence | 75

Day 18: Making God's Presence a Priority | 79

Day 19: God With Us | 84

Day 20: Occupied 'with' Christ vs. Occupied 'for' Christ | 89

Day 21: Beholding God's Glory in Jesus | 94

Day 22: God's Transforming Presence in Us | 98

Day 23: Building Blocks in God's Temple | 103

Day 24: He Will Give You Rest | 108

Day 25: Drawing Near to God through Our High Priest | 113

Day 26: Priests Who Worship in His Temple | 118

Day 27: Living in the Light of God's Presence | 123

Day 28: A Heavenly Worship Service | 128

Day 29: Who Can Stand in God's Presence? | 133

Day 30: Enjoying God's Presence Forever | 138

Works Cited | 143
Scripture Index | 145

Foreword

Dr. David Mathewson and Jennifer Fitzgerald are both deeply committed to seeking after God's presence. It shows! I have had the privilege of watching them minister to people at church services and hear glowing testimonies of encounters in God's presence from those in the small group they lead. One can easily see they live their lives from the place of intimacy with God and broker God's presence to others with whom they love and serve in community.

For me, to be around them is to see and experience His presence. When they stand near you, talk, or smile, one can easily see they have been with Jesus. They exude honor, humility, and the love of God. I would even say they emit heaven's peace as they live from this place of intimacy. And to top it off, they both have the ability to release the Holy Spirit so that others around them encounter God, touch His love, and find joy and refreshment in His presence.

This delightful devotional takes you on a 30-day journey from the head to the heart. You will travel from Genesis to Revelation reading, studying, and devotionally applying key passages that lead you to understand and encounter His Presence. I know the authors well enough to say that their goal, as they prayed over and penned these pages, is for you, the reader, to have a personal encounter with the living God. So, draw from their deep wells of intimacy with God! Receive an impartation of breakthrough as you connect with Him heart to heart! And may His Spirit take you into the gravity well of the Father's love!

Foreword

Living from God's Presence and the attendant intimate knowledge of Him is essential to produce any true fruit for the Kingdom. So many followers of Christ live only from the place of head knowledge or dutiful commitment to the Way. Cultivating intimacy with God and encounter changes all that. What was once external becomes a river of life that flows from within you (John 7:38).

Jesus Himself said all genuine ministry in the Kingdom flows from personal intimacy with God. Without it we run in danger of doing it in our strength, not His. Over and over Jesus stressed the importance of intimacy and dependency. For example, he said the following in John 14:10 (NKJV), "Don't you believe that I am in the Father and the Father is in me? The words I say to you are not just my own. Rather, it is the Father, living in me, who is doing his work." Similarly, He said in John 15:5, "I am the vine; you are the branches. If a man remains in me and I in him, he will bear much fruit; apart from me you can do nothing."

One of the greatest truths for any believer to grasp is that God Himself wants to encounter people with the full aspect of His nature and His Presence. Encounter makes theology real and what we have heard about God tangible. In fact, His presence defines us. Moses told the Lord, "If Your Presence does not go with us, do not bring us up from here. For how then will it be known that Your people and I have found grace in Your sight, except You go with us? So, we shall be separate, Your people and I, from all the people who are upon the face of the earth" (Exodus 33:15–16).

What if you, the reader, could live from a now, present encounter with the living God within you? Would it transform your insecurities if you could live with the absolute certainty that you are a loved son or daughter of God? What if you could minister to other directly from the heart of the Jesus to broker His very presence? What if the joy of the Lord really became your day-to-day strength because "in His presence is fullness of joy" (Psalm 16:11)?

Through the insights that permeate the pages that follow, you have the opportunity to experience an intimate face-to-face encounter with the very essence of God's nature and His person.

Foreword

I encourage all to read this devotional slowly and with adequate reflection. As you do, invite the Holy Spirit to release impartation to you from God's very throne room. Enjoy it and drink deeply from the river of God's presence as you embark on this journey.

Dr. Peter Young
Senior Leader, BridgeWay Church Denver, CO

Introduction

THE PURPOSE OF THIS devotional is to usher individuals into an encounter with the Living God, engaging with Him face-to-face. The intent is to experience God through our hearts, not just intellectually, thus becoming wholly devoted worshipers in spirit and in truth, transformed into His likeness.

The devotionals and meditations in this book are all unto this purpose. Scriptural truths combined with cognitive and metacognitive exercises are used to reframe and renew the mind in order to engage the heart, awaken the senses, and identify beliefs that hinder encountering the fullness of God's presence.

This devotional is designed for 30 days of consecutive reading and intentional practice of engaging the Lord and consists of two parts each day: "FROM THE HEAD" and "TO THE HEART". In the first part, "FROM THE HEAD", the emphasis is on knowledge of the Word of God and includes a Bible reading with a detailed study on the passage you just read. The section, "TO THE HEART", focuses on the practice of encountering God's presence, consisting of Reflection, Prayer, and Connection based on the passage(s) studied. There is also a blank page entitled "Notes" after each section for you to record your thoughts, prayers, and reflections. First, is the Bible reading of the passage that will be the focus of our attention as we prepare to enter God's presence. The passages that have been chosen are ones that focus on God's presence with us, from Genesis to Revelation. The Scriptures tell a story of how God created us to encounter and live in His presence.

INTRODUCTION

In fact, we suggest the primary theme of Scripture is God's intention to dwell with His people and for us to encounter His presence intimately. This thread is woven from Genesis to Revelation! Next is the Study section, with a reflection on and explanation of the passage(s) you have just read that focuses on the meaning of the passage in its context. Finally, this will be followed by an applicational section taking you beyond intellectual knowledge of the passage to applying the truths and engaging the presence of God through Meditating, Connecting, and Praying. The devotional consists of 30 studies to be read in a month, one devotional for each day.

If the idea of cultivating an experiential and heart knowledge of God is uncomfortable or seems to verge on emotionalism or weakness, consider the following. In Luke 10:27, Jesus was asked what the greatest commandment is, He answered, "To love the Lord your God with all your heart, all your soul, all your strength and all your mind." The term "heart" in this passage is used to mean the vigor of physical life, or the seat of passions, desires, appetites, affections, purposes and endeavors. Heart, in this regard, is used numerous times in Scripture. Take Rom 10:9-10: "If you confess with your mouth Jesus is Lord and believe in your heart that God raised Him from the dead, you will be saved." How many of us believe with our minds, yet our hearts (the source of our strongest passion, most desperate appetite and fiery affection) is disconnected from God? It is belief from the *heart* that brings salvation. Jesus again spoke to this in Matt 15:8: "These people honor me with their lips, but their hearts are far from me." He went on to say there are those that know the Scriptures, and they worship Him in vain, as they are merely following a bunch of rules without intimate relationship based on love.

God wants to know you intimately, and He longs for us to experience Him with our whole being, including our emotions, not just an intellectual knowledge of Him.

If you are willing to lay aside judgements of emotionalism and preconceived ideas of a distant God, you are invited to step into an unfathomable, unlimited relationship of experiential knowledge

INTRODUCTION

of the fullness of God's presence that surpasses only your mind to become rooted in your heart.

If engaging with God's presence is a new concept, or if you are unfamiliar with the term 'God's presence' and desire to experience Him in a deeper way, we encourage you to set aside the next 30 days to do just that. We are promised in Scripture that if we seek God, we will find Him. Set your mind for the next month to seek Him with your whole heart, knock and keep knocking- be persistent! I promise, He will answer. That is a guarantee. He promises He is a rewarder of those who seek Him.

Below are simple prayers to pray every day over the next month. Ask, seek and knock, and the door will be opened.

1. Pray daily for an increase of hunger for Him and His Word.

2. Surrender daily and submit to His leadership over your mind, your heart, your soul, your body, and your spirit.

3. Pray for the eyes of your heart to see him rightly and for a tenderized heart and sensitized spirit.

4. Pray for clean hands and a pure heart, that beliefs or behaviors that hinder the full experience of His presence would be revealed.

5. Ask Holy Spirit to pour Himself out over you, however it looks, whatever it takes.

Get ready, friend. He's coming for you!

Day 1

It Begins with Delight

FROM THE HEAD...

Read: Genesis 2:4–14; 3:8

Study

The starting point for understanding God's presence in Scripture is the creation account in Gen 1–2. Genesis 1 outlines the seven-day creative act of God where simply by His powerful, spoken word He brought everything into existence. During separate days he brought into existence land, bodies of water, sky, light, plants, animals, and the pinnacle of his creative work, man and woman (Adam and Eve). When we read Gen 1, we might be tempted to merely see an account of the origin of our world, and not much else. How did this planet, the universe, and human beings come into existence? However, there is so much more to discover than that.

First, God is creating a beautiful place, not just suitable for humans to live, but an abundant oasis in which man can delight and where he can be in relationship with Him. A place without light and plants would not be a habitable place for the people God created. Secondly, and more importantly, as Gen 2:4–14 especially shows, God is creating the Garden of Eden to be a place where He can manifest His presence with Adam and Eve. The garden is to be a sanctuary where God can dwell with His people He created. Specific elements of this first creation account, the garden-sanctuary, will appear later in the Old Testament in the construction of the tabernacle and temple: Plants (the plants carved on the walls of the temple), and light (the candelabra in the holy place), the tree of life (the golden lampstand). God is creating a temple, a sacred space, because he intends to reveal his presence with his people. He desires that we experience intimate encounters with Him.

The garden of Eden was a place of fruitfulness, abundance, and life. There was a river that flowed from the garden giving life and abundance to the land, just as a river flowed out of the temple in Ezek 47. Gold was in the garden, as there was overlaid gold in most of the tabernacle and temple. Gold symbolized beauty and purity. It also symbolized God's presence. God places Adam in the garden to "*work* it and *take care* of it" (v. 15). These two words are used later of the priests' duties in the tabernacle (Num 3:7–8; 8:26; 18:5–6). Adam is not the first gardener; he is the first priest! Two cherubim guarded the entrance to the garden, just like the two cherubim who watched over the Ark in the Holy of Holies. As a place of divine presence, God regularly walked in the garden (Gen 3:8): "Then the man and his wife heard the sound of the Lord God as he was walking in the garden in the cool of the day." The garden was meant to be a temple, a sanctuary, a place of encounter. This shows how the very first chapters of the Bible reveal God's heart and original intention for his people: To enjoy and experience God's presence, a close relationship with their Creator, through intimate encounters with Him in this sacred space. However, as the story unfolds, in Gen 3 Adam and Eve bring sin into the sanctuary where God's presence dwelt, and they had to be removed from the Garden-temple. God cannot dwell in the presence of sin. Sin is the greatest barrier to experiencing the fullness of God's presence and intimate encounters with Him. The rest of Scripture after Gen 3 could be seen as the story of how God is going to restore his presence with His people. How will God once again live with His people? How will they once more experience intimate encounters with His presence?

...TO THE HEART

Meditate

Eden in Hebrew is defined as a 'place of pleasure, a garden of delight or bliss'.

What implication does this have for us when we encounter God? Why do you think God chose this place to encounter Him? What does this say about the nature of the relationship He desires? What does this say about His nature? What truth about God can I take away to build a foundation for engaging with His heart?

Connect

If the Garden of Eden was a place where God dwelt with people, where does this take place today under the New Covenant? Connecting your heart with God's heart also requires engaging your feelings. Take a few minutes and remember the first time you felt God's overwhelming love for you. Recall what it felt like, and how your perspective shifted. This is the same delight God created you to experience when coming before Him. Write out your desire to know God experientially, to delight in Him, and to know His delight for you.

Pray

Ask God to awaken your first love with Him again. Pray these verses from the Psalms over your heart in the first person:

> Ps 36:8-9: "They will be abundantly satisfied with the fatness of Your house; and You will make them drink of the river of Your pleasures. For with You is the fountain of life: in your light we will see light."

> Ps 16:11: "You will show me the path of life: in your Presence is fullness of joy; at Your right hand there are pleasures forevermore."

THIRTY DAYS IN GOD'S PRESENCE

Notes:

Day 2

Entering in through the Tabernacle

FROM THE HEAD...

Read: Exodus 25:8–9; 29:44–46; 40:34–38

Study:

The purpose of God bringing Abraham to a land promised to him (Gen 12:1–2) was to restore His presence that was lost in the Garden of Eden. God desired His children to once more experience intimate encounters with Him. We see this being fulfilled in the book of Exodus. The goal of our salvation is that we experience the presence of God. However, God does not wait for the Israelites to arrive in their Promised Land to reveal Himself to His people. After God delivers them from Egypt (Exod 1–15), He leads them through the wilderness to the land God promised Abraham and his descendants. On their journey through the wilderness, a tent-like structure known as a tabernacle is where people would encounter God's presence. The tabernacle would accompany Israel on their trek to the promised land. It was a temporary "temple" that could be set up and taken down on their journey. This is the first major step in God restoring his presence with His people from Gen 1–2. You can read all the details regarding the blueprint and building of the tabernacle in Exod 25–40. Almost one half of

Exodus is devoted to the tabernacle, which reveals the value and priority God places on it!

The word "Tabernacle" is a translation of the Hebrew word *mishkan*, which means "tent" or "dwelling." The tabernacle consisted of three main parts: The outer court, the Holy Place, and the Holy of Holies. It is this third place, the Holy of Holies, where God's presence resided, the most intimate place of encounter. The climax of the description of the tabernacle is when God's presence comes to fill it: "Then the cloud covered the Tent of Meeting, and the glory of the Lord filled the tabernacle. Moses could not enter the tent of meeting because the cloud had settled upon it, and the glory of the Lord filled the tabernacle" (Exod 40:34–35). The glory of the Lord that Adam and Eve lost access to can now be experienced once again. However, there was a catch in experiencing the presence of God in the tabernacle. Only the high priest could enter the Holy of Holies, which was where God encountered His people, and then only once a year. If you weren't a priest, you were restricted to the outer court. The way for *everyone* to enter the Holy of Holies, which was where God's Presence manifested, awaited the coming of Christ (Heb 4, 9–10). The tabernacle only served to anticipate something greater, a closer encounter with God's presence.

An important feature of the tabernacle we have already noticed is its numerous correspondences to the Garden of Eden in Gen 2. Like the first creation, light illuminated the Holy Place. Like the gold in the Garden of Eden, gold played a key role in the construction of the tabernacle. It symbolized beauty and purity, but more importantly divine presence. Like the tree of life in the Garden, there was a seven-branched tree-shaped lampstand in the temple. Like the plants and trees in the Garden, there were plants and trees engraved on the walls of the tabernacle. Like the two angels that guarded the entrance to the Garden, two Cherubim watched over the ark in the Holy of Holies, the place where God met with His people. What is the point? The tabernacle was meant to be a miniature Garden of Eden. God was restoring his presence with His people which was lost at the Garden, creating a place where his children could experience intimate encounters with Him. God takes seriously encountering His people; and so must they.

...TO THE HEART

Meditate

In the New Covenant, we are the tabernacle. As I Cor 6:19 tells us, our bodies are the temple of the Holy Spirit. With this imagery, let's encounter God through an exercise using the Old Testament model of the tabernacle as our 'map'. The structure of the Old Testament tabernacle consisted of an outer court with the altar of sacrifice, an inner court with the altar of incense, and the inner room, the Holy of Holies containing the mercy seat. If our bodies are the temple of the Holy Spirit, let's look at our bodies as a representation of the temple. The outer court represents our flesh, this is where we offer the sacrifice of praise. The inner court represents our soul, where we engage in prayer that becomes a fragrant offering before the Lord. The Holy of Holies, reserved just for the priest, the most sacred and intimate of places, is our spirit. This is where we commune with God spirit-to-spirit.

As you begin this exercise in the Pray portion, understand it requires a directing of your will; you are training your appetites, rewiring your mind to engage with God's Spirit. Don't allow distractions in the outer courts to sidetrack you from your pursuit; you must push through beyond the flesh. Ps 63:4-5 shows the progression of one who seeks God's face in His sanctuary: Hands uplifted in praise, an overflow of His lovingkindness bursts forth, and your soul deeply satisfied as with abundant 'fatness'. Sometimes it comes as a warmth, a depth of being known and loved, feeling completely alive, and your spirit stirred. As you progress through the stages, you may feel a weight of His glory that makes it difficult to physically move. Your mind is alert to hear the Lord's voice clearly without question. Praise and adoration overflow from your heart. You lose track of time and feel like you could stay in this place all day. Everything else pales in comparison, as you have His thoughts and His perspective.

Pray

Psalm 100:4 gives us the first step to entering the Holy of Holies through the outer courts: "Enter into His gates with thanksgiving, and into his courts with praise: Be thankful to him and bless his name." Enter in the outer courts by thanking God for who He is and what He has done for you. In this step, be as specific as possible. As you engage your heart with gratitude, speak out loud, lift your voice! This is the stage where we leave behind the cares of the world, the fleshly distractions. You may find this to be difficult at first. Just keep your eyes on Jesus and press through. Once you notice your emotions are engaged and your spirit is stirred, move on to the inner courts.

The inner court symbolizes our soul, which consists of mind, heart and will. Your soul speaks of thoughts, imaginations, desires, passions, and choices. In this step, your emotions are engaged and you will continue 'directing your soul', as David speaks of in Psalms. The goal is to find your delight in the Lord. Direct your soul by surrendering in whole-hearted abandoned consecration of heart, mind, and body to the Lord. Lay out the pieces of your life on the altar by visually and verbally placing your protective walls, defenses, offenses, judgements, trauma, pain, questions, expectations, plans, fears, and all else on the altar one by one. Entwine your heart with His in full surrender, entrusting Him with every part of your life. Wait silently on the Lord and allow Holy Spirit to ignite your heart. You may hear nothing and feel nothing. Stay in this place until your spirit is awakened. This can feel like you are strengthened within, or filled with peace, or your affections are stirred for the Lord with tears or overwhelming love. If distracted, continue to praise the Lord.

The next progression is to proceed into the Holy of Holies. This represents spirit-to-spirit communion with God, the secret place of personal intimate relationship with God. God is Spirit, and we engage with Him through our spirit. His Spirit will give life to our bodies as we behold the glory of the Lord and are transformed into His image through the Spirit. The experience of this stage is 'overflow'. If the outer court represents a filling of your cup, the inner court is a full cup, the Holy of Holies is the overflow of your cup. You are fully engaged with your spirit, listening and seeing with the eyes of your spirit rather than the soul or inclinations dictated by the flesh. This is where the mercy seat is located, where we are commanded to come boldly before the Lord in Hebrews 10 and cry out 'Abba Father' (Gal 4:6).

Connect

Use this blueprint to engage your spirit as a walking tabernacle. Be vigilant to guard this time as if your life depends on it! When we encounter the Living God we all together realize how desperately our real life depends on daily communing with Him. This is the antidote to living in survival mode, constantly worn out and distracted from heaven's realities. Learn to live from God's presence as He supercharges our life and energizes our spirit. He fills us with His love, empowering us to walk in the spirit as we abide in Him and bring His kingdom to earth around us!

THIRTY DAYS IN GOD'S PRESENCE
Notes:

Day 3

Becoming a Fragrant Incense

FROM THE HEAD...

Read: Exodus 30:1–10

Study

God commanded Moses to build a tabernacle, a portable 'temple', that would accompany Israel in their journey through the wilderness and would begin to restore God's intention to live in the midst of His people as He had in the Garden of Eden. This tabernacle contained a number of important pieces of furniture in it, such as the Table of the Bread of Presence, or the Golden Lampstand that illuminated the Most Holy Place, and each one had a particular importance and function for bringing God's presence to the people. An important piece of furniture found in the tabernacle was the Altar of Incense. It was a wooden 'box' that stood right in front of the entrance to the Holy of Holies, which housed the Ark of the Covenant where God met with His people. The fact that it is right next to the Holy of Holies, the most intimate place of encounter with God, points to its importance. Its dimensions and construction are described in detail in Exod 30:1–11. It was made of a certain type of wood, Acacia wood. This square-shaped altar was overlaid with gold. There were gold rings on the corners so that you could put wooden poles through the rings in order to carry it. There were also four golden horns, one on each corner of the altar. Like every other piece of furniture in the tabernacle, no expense was spared in constructing this altar, which stood before the curtain that separated off the Holy of Holies.

But what did this altar do? Why was it there? We have already noted that it is right in front of the entrance to the place God will meet with His people, the Holy of Holies. This passage from Exodus tells us that the priest, Aaron, is to burn fragrant incense on this altar every day, in the morning and then again in the evening. That is a lot of incense - two times a day for 360+ days a year! It was to be an offering to the Lord, and it was to be perpetual, meaning that it would burn all the time. Then once a year, on the Day of Atonement, Aaron was to place blood on the four horns of the altar in order to cleanse it and make atonement, making it most holy to the Lord. The incense altar seems to be preparatory for entering into the Holy of Holies, the meeting place with God. This is why it is placed right in front of the entrance into the Holy of Holies. But what is the significance of incense? The incense is meant to represent prayers that rise up to God. In other places in Scripture incense represents the prayers of God's people. Ps 141:2 says: "May my prayer be set before you like incense." Twice in the book of Revelation incense symbolizes the prayers of the saints. In Rev 5:8 the four living creatures hold "golden bowls full of incense, which is the prayer of the saints." And in Rev 8:3-4 an angel is given "much incense to offer, with the prayers of all the saints on the golden altar before the throne [the altar of incense in heaven!]. The smoke of the incense, together with the prayers of the saints, went up before God." So the altar of incense represented the prayers of the priest as he entered the Holy of Holies. What is important about the altar of incense? The way that God's people are to come into His presence is through prayer and praise. Prayer is a priestly act that ushers us into an encounter with the holy God, but it is prayer done with a sincere heart which is a pleasing fragrance to Him.

...TO THE HEART
Meditate

If prayer and praise usher us into God's Presence, understanding these terms as God defines them is crucial. Look up both terms in a Old Testament word study, or access one online at biblehub.com and write it down. The Psalmist declares in Ps 141:2, "Let my prayer be set before You as incense, the lifting up of my hands as the evening sacrifice." What is the difference between prayer and praise? What are some characteristics of praise? How do you offer up a sacrifice? Now read Ps 40:6. Define the sacrifice God is looking for. This verse is also used by the author of Hebrews in context of entering into the Holy of Holies (Heb 10:5–7). How are these two verses from the Psalms related? How can this be implemented in your own life as you enter into the Holy of Holies?

Pray

Begin communing with God through praise. Write a Psalm of your own to the Lord. Include three aspects of God's character or attributes you have personally experienced. Begin and end your Psalm telling Him of your love for Him. Let adoration flow from a fountain of gratitude. Recall His love and grace over your life, what He has saved you from, and how He encountered you along the way. Close your Psalm with promises He has spoken to you from the Word.

Connect

Our journey's destination isn't to just encounter Him and then proceed with our day. The destination is Him and to abide in Him throughout our day. Once we connect with Him through worship, the goal is to maintain this spirit-to-spirit communing, keeping that fire stoked and lit! Sustaining the attitude of worship helps support the internal state of abiding, keeping your incense burning.

Notes:

Day 4

Resting in God's Presence

FROM THE HEAD...

Read: Exodus 33:14–16

Study

We have already noted that nearly one-half of the book of Exodus is devoted to the description and building of the tabernacle. This shows the importance of God's presence with His people, not only in the book of Exodus, but in the entire Bible. The climax of the account of Moses building the tabernacle is the awesome scene where God's presence enters the completed tabernacle. The intention of God rescuing His people out of Egypt is so that He could dwell with them! Deliverance was for the purpose of dwelling. That is the story of Exodus.

But the story takes an unfortunate turn. Despite the fact that God has just delivered the people from Egypt, they are now witnessing the building of the tabernacle where God will dwell with the people, but decide to construct an idol, a golden calf that they will worship, in Exod 32. You would think that after all they witnessed when God brought them out of Egypt, this would not even be a temptation. But sin and idolatry were lurking just below the surface waiting to lead God's people astray. If God's people are not diligent to steward God's presence, sin can easily enter in. The nation of Israel gave in. As a consequence for their idolatry, God removes His presence from the people. This was the reason God removed Adam and Eve from His presence in the Garden of Eden in Gen 3: Sin. And now God's people sin again, once more resulting in the removal of God's presence. God then instructs Moses that He will send an angel to guide the people into the promised land God would give them, but God Himself will not go with them as they make their journey to the land (Exod 33:2–3).

Moses then reacts to this news by approaching and pleading with God for His glorious presence to lead him. It would not be enough for *an angel* to lead him and the Israelites (33:2). Moses wanted nothing less than God's very presence to go with him. It is interesting that God was still meeting with Moses in a tent, known as the 'tent of meeting' (33:7–11). Moses would pitch this tent outside of the Israelite camp, where he would go to inquire of the Lord. The pillar of cloud, a sign of God's presence that followed Israel through the wilderness, would come down to the entrance of the tent: "As Moses went into the tent, the pillar of cloud would come down and stay at the entrance, while the Lord spoke with Moses" (33:9). So Moses was still able to experience God's presence in the special place of encounter. In fact, his encounter with the presence of God was described with the intimate language of "face to face" (33:11). But this was not enough. It was not enough for Moses to occasionally encounter God's presence when he went into the tent. He desired God's presence to accompany him into the promised land, to be with him at all times.

God responds to Moses by promising that His presence will indeed go with him and the people: "My presence will go with you, and I will give you rest" (33:14). Notice God's presence and rest are associated here. The rest God promised to give Moses was the rest He would give them when He brought them into the land where He would dwell with them. Notice Moses' response: "If your presence does not go with us, do not send us up from here" (33:15). At that moment God allowed Moses to get a glimpse of His very glory (33:18–23). God's intention for His people was that they experience rest that comes from abiding in the very presence of God.

This rest in God's presence was intended to point to something greater. In Heb 3-4 (on this passage see below) we are told that this rest is still available today for us. We now experience that rest in God's presence in the person of Jesus Christ. We encounter God's presence by resting in Christ, who is the very radiance of the glory of God that Moses only got to glimpse.

...TO THE HEART

Meditate

In the divine scheme of Israel's deliverance, God's purpose was to dwell with them. God's intention is that deliverance brings about freedom for the purpose of dwelling in God's presence unhindered. Trace the theme of God's hand of deliverance in your own life. Consider what you have been delivered from, and what you were delivered unto. God delivers, but what we are delivered unto is determined by our decisions. What choices have you made and are still making? What is the fruit? What happened with the Israelites after their deliverance? What did God withhold as a result of their choices? How did the Israelites respond? How was Joshua different and where did he spend his time? What were the effects of his choices?

Pray

As you meditate on today's passage, what stands out to you? Talk about this with the Lord. Is your hunger stirred for His presence? Do you want the same hunger and see the same need that Moses had for God's presence to go with him? Ask God to awaken and increase your hunger. Ask Holy Spirit to highlight areas that need to be re-consecrated to the Lord in your life.

Connect

What would it look like for you to abide in God's presence? Sit with the Lord and imagine His presence filling your life and going with you about your day.

Notes:

Day 5

Priests in God's Service

FROM THE HEAD...

Read: Leviticus 9:1–7, 23–24

Study

We see the first place God chose to manifest His presence was in the tabernacle after they were removed from His presence in the Garden of Eden. After Moses built the tabernacle, the glory of God's presence filled it. But for God's presence to remain with the people, there were certain requirements they had to maintain. An important part of the functioning of the tabernacle to house God's presence was the service of the priests. We have already seen in Exodus that only the high priest could enter the Holy of Holies, the place of the most intimate encounter with God, and then only once a year. It was closed off to him the rest of the year. Basically, the purpose of the priest was to mediate the presence of God to the people. Not just anyone could stroll into the Holy of Holies whenever they felt like it! The priest represented the people before God. He was sort of a mediator or 'go-between' for the people and the presence of God. The priest would offer sacrifices for the sins of the people, but also for himself. He would also bless the people and ensure the holiness of God's dwelling place.

Priests in God's Service

Not just anyone could serve as a priest. No one could wake up one morning and decide, "I think I would like to become a priest! I would love to serve in the temple, and I really like the priestly robes!" No, you had to be in the right family line, the line of Aaron. Only then could you serve as a priest and perform the priestly duties. Leviticus 8–9 is about the consecration of Aaron and his sons to be priests and the beginning of their ministry in the tabernacle. The consecration and ordination of Aaron and his sons takes place in chapter 8, and it was quite a ceremony! Everything was cleansed and all the required offerings were made. After their consecration, in chapter 9, the priests prepare the people for the appearance of the Lord in their midst. The priests must offer sacrifices for both themselves and the people, because "today the Lord will appear to you" (v. 4); their burnt offerings were "so that the glory of the Lord may appear to you" (v. 6). God could only appear to His people and dwell in their midst if everything was purified. As we saw in Gen 3, it was sin that barred Adam and Eve from God's presence. In Lev 9 the numerous sacrifices, the sin offering, the burnt offering, and the fellowship offering, were all necessary to deal with the sin that stood between humanity and God. In this the priests were to follow carefully everything that God commanded them. Approaching the presence of God was not a casual or lighthearted matter. It was to be treated with the utmost care and seriousness.

After the priests had performed their duties of offering up sacrifices on behalf of themselves and the people, they blessed the people, and the glory of the Lord appeared so they encountered the presence of God. As a result, they fell down on the ground and shouted with joy at the appearance of God's glory in their midst in verses 23–24. So the priests were absolutely necessary if God was to dwell with His people. Yet we will see that the priesthood and the sacrifices in the Old Testament were only a shadow of a greater reality. With the coming of Jesus everything changes: Jesus himself would be our priest who offered Himself as a sacrifice for our sins so we can approach God (Heb 9–10). He also makes all of us to be priests (1 Pet 2), those who approach God's presence, worship

Him, and offer sacrifices of praise and worship. What an amazing privilege!

...TO THE HEART

Meditate

In light of today's passage, read Heb 7:18–19. Where does God choose to manifest His presence today? Where is the tabernacle in the New Covenant? What was the role of the priest? Who is our High Priest and what does that mean for you today when you approach God? Read 1 Pet 2:9 and meditate on what it means to be set apart and appointed as God's priest. What does it look like to be a priest for God?

Pray

Begin by thanking Jesus for His sacrifice to allow you to enter into God's presence. Allow your heart to get caught in the delight of Jesus' love for you. Express this love to Him. As you take communion in the Connect portion below, listen to Him speak to you as you engage with Him face to face.

Connect

Take communion, and as you take the bread and drink, recognize Jesus' sacrifice and His role as your mediator to open the door for you to enter God's presence. As you take communion, take a physical step 'into' the Holy of Holies, seeing yourself In Christ and Him in you.

Notes:

Day 6

God's Name and God's Dwelling

FROM THE HEAD...

Read: Deuteronomy 12:5–7

Study

The people of Israel were preparing to enter their promised land, after He had led them out of Egypt. Adam and Eve had lost the "land", the garden and place of God's presence, and now God was going to give His people a land where he would once more live with them. These verses in Deuteronomy are a reminder of the importance of establishing a place of God's presence. When the people of Israel arrive in the land that God would give them, it would be occupied by a foreign nation, the Canaanites, and their pagan temples and gods. So, verses 1–4 commands the Israelites to get rid of them to prepare a way for God's dwelling. God cannot dwell among pagan gods. There can be no other gods before him (Exod 20:3), and if God is to dwell in the land it must be pure and vacant of all foreign, ungodly influences. The presence of God that accompanied the Israelites on their trek through the desert would now come to rest in the new land God was giving them. In verses 5–7 Moses commands the people to seek the place God would choose for His presence to dwell. This demonstrates the utmost importance of God's presence with the people; it is a priority. It also shows the purpose of God is not that they can own a piece of real estate, but that He can dwell with them, just as He did in the Garden of Eden. Encountering God's *presence* in the *place* of God's choosing!

Why are the people of God commanded to put God's name there as His dwelling (v. 5)? The "Name" indicates God's intention for us to encounter Him personally and intimately; that is why he places His name to dwell in their midst. God is jealous for His people and wants to live with them. That is why anything else, gods and idols, that would compete, or interfere, must be completely removed (vv. 1–4). The other response of God's people in God's presence is sacrifice, praise, and worship. Verse 5 tells the people "there [at the place of God's dwelling], bring your burnt offerings and sacrifices, your tithes and special gifts, what you have vowed to give and your freewill offerings, and the firstborn from your herds and flocks." Nothing less than the best is acceptable in the powerful presence of God.

Being in God's presence should also be a time of celebrating and rejoicing: "There in the presence of the Lord your God, you and your families shall eat and shall rejoice in everything you have put your hand to" (v. 7). Notice there is a progression in this passage: Preparation for encountering God's presence by removing all that competes or hinders; then engaging through worship and sacrifice; finally, rejoicing and celebrating in God's presence. God's intention is that we all experience the all-consuming presence of God. God, and His people, will not be satisfied with anything less.

...TO THE HEART
Meditate

Why did God command removal of all idols? If an idol is defined as anything that competes with, or separates us from our affection for Jesus, consider what cultural idols currently affect your heart? Where does the affection of your heart rest? Read Ps 97:10.

Consider what is allowed into your home via phone, computer, TV, and what has captured the gaze of your affection. Think about your last two weeks and write down what you have turned to for comfort when overwhelmed, stressed, lonely, or bored. Now consider practical ways you can train the appetite of your affections towards Jesus.

Pray

Read Ps 119:37 and Ps 37:4–7. Pray these back to the Lord in the first person. Commit specific ways to exchange these areas for turning your affection to Him. Re-dedicate yourself, your home, and your family to the Lord in every area of your day. As you draw near to Him, He will draw near to you!

Connect

Take the areas you wrote down from the Meditate exercise and make a plan to modify your behavior. Begin by committing small increments of your day to meditating on His love or reading a Psalm, particularly when you are feeling the pull towards counterfeit satiation. This is interrupting the accustomed path to temporary comfort by establishing new pathways to help focus your desires and affections on Jesus.

Notes:

Day 7

A Home for God's Presence

FROM THE HEAD...

Read: 1 Kings 8:10–13

Study

The next stopping point in our study of the presence of God is the temple in Jerusalem. God's people are now settled in the land God gave them, and the city of Jerusalem is central, sort of the "capitol" city. The tabernacle of God's presence that accompanied Israel in the wilderness finally finds a more permanent resting place in the temple in Jerusalem. The tabernacle was a temporary temple, and the temple is a permanent tabernacle! It was Israel's king and David's son, Solomon, who was responsible for constructing the temple. You can read the story of its design and construction in great detail in 1 Kgs 5–8, resembling the design and construction of the tabernacle in Exod 25–40. Similar to the tabernacle, the temple consisted of three main sections: The outer court, the Holy Place, and the Holy of Holies. The latter room is where the ark of the covenant rested and where God manifested his immediate presence with His people. Like the tabernacle, the temple was where God's intimate presence was manifested, yet still restricted the presence of God. Only priests could enter the outer room, the Holy Place.

The most intimate encounter with God was reserved for the Holy of Holies. The Holy of Holies is where the ark of the covenant was and where God met with the High Priest. Only the high priest upon proper purification could enter the Holy of Holies, and only once a year on the Day of Atonement. A further restriction is that only Israel had access to God's presence through the temple. This was also only a shadow of better things to come, when everyone would one day have direct access to God's presence through their high priest, Jesus Christ (see the book of Hebrews).

We can also see that like the tabernacle, the temple was meant to be a miniature Garden of Eden. It was covered with gold, a symbol of God's presence; plants, palm trees, and cherubim were engraved on its walls, indicating life and fruitfulness; two cherubim guarded the ark of the covenant in the Holy of Holies; a "tree" (golden lampstand) gave light to the Holy Place. The lamp signified the illumination of God's presence. The other piece of furniture, the table of the Bread of Presence, by its name indicates the importance of the temple: It is a place where people feast on and partake of the presence of God. The construction of the temple was a further step in God's intention to make His presence known to His people so they could experience intimate encounters with the Lord. The climax of the description of the temple and its construction is found in 1 Kgs 8:10-13, when the glory of the Lord filled the finished temple: "When the priests withdrew from the Holy Place, the cloud filled the temple of the Lord [just like it did the tabernacle]. And the priests could not perform their service because of the cloud, for the glory of the Lord filled His temple. Then Solomon said, 'The Lord has said that he will dwell in a dark cloud. I have indeed built a magnificent temple for You, a place for You to dwell forever.'" God's intention for us is that we experience the close presence of God, in intimate encounters with Him. This is what we were created for, and the temple demonstrates the importance of encountering God's presence. We are now His temple.

It also reveals the heart of God: He desires to dwell with us, and to experience intimate encounters with Him.

...TO THE HEART

Meditate

How does the Garden of Eden relate to the temple? What happened in the garden before sin? What happened in the Holy of Holies that didn't happen in the outer courts? Write down feelings that come to mind when you think of encountering God in the Holy of Holies or engaging with Him at this intimate level every day. What beliefs do your feelings point to? Submit each one to God and ask Holy Spirit to reveal what beliefs, or lies, you are holding onto that hinder you from encountering God in the secret place. Turn away from each one and ask Holy Spirit to give you Scriptural truths that refute these beliefs. Write down these Scriptures. For example, if anxiety and doubt rise up when engaging the Lord, ask yourself why you feel anxiety and what you are doubting. If the thought comes to mind, 'I won't hear God speak, He isn't going to encounter me, or this is just my imagination', write these down. Then find Scripture that addresses each belief, such as John 10:27 or Ps 40:6–10, for questioning God speaking, or Heb 3–4 and 11:1–2 for addressing unbelief and doubt. Meditate on these passages until the belief is uprooted and exchanged with truth. Allow these truths to uproot lies, and then walk through the tabernacle model of engaging your spirit with the Lord now strengthened in faith!

Pray

After taking the above beliefs and submitting them to the Lordship of Christ, engage your heart in worship. Tell the Lord your desire to make yourself His home. Express your love and adoration to Him. Thank Him for the truths He has given you to declare over your heart. Thank Him for His presence.

Connect

We were created to come boldly into the Holy of Holies with a clean conscience and abide in this place daily. The enemy's goal is to hinder us from this by exchanging Biblical truths for lies. We must take every thought captive so we can boldly enter!

Notes:

Day 8

Who Can Approach God's Presence?

FROM THE HEAD...

Read: Psalm 15

Study

Psalms were the worship music of the Israelites. At the heart of worship, God's people encounter His presence. It is a two-way street: We encounter His presence in worship, and worship is how we encounter His presence. Therefore, it should not surprise us to see numerous Psalms celebrating the presence of God and the central role of God's temple in the life of the people. The Psalms lead us into the presence of God in worship to Him. The primary way we encounter God is through our worship. One important theme we find in Psalms is that the presence of God requires worshippers who are holy, while at the same time His presence transforms the lives of those who experience it. Ps 15 begins with a question: "Lord, who may dwell in your sanctuary? Who may live on your holy hill?" That is, what kind of person can approach and have access to God's presence? The rest of this Psalm answers the question by describing the person who is qualified to have access to intimacy with God in His temple. In fact, the Psalm was probably sung by Israel in preparation for entering the temple. I believe it is also describing the person who is transformed by encountering the presence of God.

If you remember back in the Garden of Eden it was sin that banned Adam and Eve from the Garden-temple. They were no longer able to enjoy the immediate presence of God. In the same way, Ps 15 is a reminder of the incompatibility of sin with entering into the presence of God. What is required of those who would enter God's presence? Entering God's presence requires a transformed, pure life and righteous behavior in conformity with the character of the God whose presence we approach:

- They must be holy and blameless in word and in deed.
- They do not speak evil of others, gossip, or slander.
- They are fair in their dealings with others.
- They are characterized by justice, by mercy, and by integrity.

Nothing less is required of those who would approach God in worship. The Psalm ends by reminding us that such a person will not be shaken. They will find peace and security in God's presence. Experiencing intimacy with God requires preparation, being holy and righteous before the Lord. God's presence cannot tolerate sin. Entering into God's presence through worship cannot be taken lightly or treated carelessly. We see the words God has for his people in Mal 1 when they do not bring the best to be sacrificed, when they offered blemished and diseased animals: This was showing contempt for the Lord, it was an abomination, it was profane, and the person who brings such useless sacrifices is profane. God requires that we bring the very best to Him when we approach His presence in worship. We are the living sacrifices (Rom 12:1–2). We must be pure, unblemished, and holy. Yet at the same time, experiencing God's presence has a transforming effect. We cannot achieve on our own the righteousness and holiness that God requires. We cannot earn our way into God's presence through good works. But encountering God's presence will transform and renew us to be the people that God desires to dwell with.

...TO THE HEART

Meditate

It is possible to experience measures of God's presence and glory corporately, as in the outer courts. However, there remains significantly more for those wholly consecrated, who live in accordance to His Word in purity with clean hands and a pure heart and enter the Holy of Holies. Our relationship transforms as we abide in Him. If thanksgiving is the gate to the outer courts of the temple, consecration and holiness is the way into the Holy of Holies. Read 1 John 3:20–21. In light of Ps 15 and 1 John 3, what preparation needs to take place in your own life to ascend the hill of the Lord?

Pray

Begin by delighting yourself in the Lord. Once your delight and focus is on Him, surrender your heart, thoughts, intentions, and motives to Him. Wait on the Lord and see if anything comes to mind. Thank Him for purifying you. Spend time listening to Him and respond to what He highlights.

Connect

Remember, this is a life-long sojourn into abiding and ascending. There is no final destination, so to speak; it is a relationship. You can always ascend higher. This is a cultivated process that takes us deeper and deeper into a constantly growing intimate relationship with His heart!

Notes:

Day 9

Climbing the Lord's Holy Hill

FROM THE HEAD...

Read: Psalm 24:3–10

Study

Psalm 24 celebrates the Lord's entrance into Zion, the hill of the Lord, the place of His sanctuary in Jerusalem. Psalm 24 may have been written to celebrate when David brought the ark of the covenant to Jerusalem (see 2 Sam 6 for this event). It closely resembles Ps 15 in giving requirements for those who would approach the presence of God: "Who may ascend to the hill of the Lord? Who may stand in His holy place?" (v. 3). That is, what is required of those who would encounter God and worship in His presence? The next verse answers this question: God requires complete holiness of those who would approach Him. He requires pure hands and a pure heart. There is no room for idols, or inappropriate speech that lacks integrity. God is holy, and therefore He requires holiness of those who would come in contact with His presence. This is what God requires of those "who seek your face, O God of Jacob." To seek His face means to seek after and experience the personal presence of God. At the same time, since no one is without sin, those who seek His face cannot help but be purified and transformed by time in His presence.

These verses can be seen as a preparation for what comes in the rest of the Psalm (vv. 7–10). In these verses, the presence of the Lord now enters the city. Notice the repetition of the title "King of glory." It occurs five times in these verses. God's glory that filled the Garden of Eden, and the tabernacle in the wilderness, now comes to fill the city of Jerusalem and the temple. God who is king over His people now comes to dwell among His worshippers. Even the gates and doors are pictured metaphorically as welcoming and rejoicing in the arrival of God's glorious presence. How much more should God's people welcome and rejoice in the glorious presence of the Lord. Notice again the connection between verses 3–6 and 7–10. In preparation for the arrival of God's glorious presence, His people are to prepare themselves by making sure their hands are clean and their hearts are pure. If God's people are to experience increasing measures of His presence, they must prepare for it with lives that reflect His holiness.

As we saw with Ps 15, sin kept Adam and Eve from experiencing the presence of God. In the same way it is sin that keeps us from experiencing and enjoying Him. God takes approaching His presence seriously; and so must His people. We are fellowshipping with the Lord almighty, the King of glory! This is not something that we manufacture on our own; it is not a works-based righteousness; it is not an attempt to earn the favor of God and the blessing of His presence. Rather, a transformed life comes as a response to God's grace, and God's transforming presence. If we do have sin, the beauty of the gospel is that we come straight to Him and He will cleanse us from all unrighteousness. God's presence and grace are not an excuse to sin but should motivate us to holy living.

...TO THE HEART

Meditate

This passage is an open invitation to come into the Holy of Holies. God is giving us directions into the secret place (Ps 91:1). It begins with a glimpse of His majesty, focusing our eyes on the King of Kings, the subject of this passage. He is the One who created the world, who fills heaven and earth, who pushed back the ocean, and who claims you as His own. In light of this, the question to ask is, 'Who can dare draw near to Him and stand in His Holy place?' Not everyone who claims a relationship with Him abides here. This is a conditional invitation to experience an ever-increasing dimension of His glory and indwelling presence. However, the invitation requires a response. What are the conditions of the invitation? How do individual choices and actions impact the measure of intimacy, or promise of ascending to His holy mountain according to this passage? Read James 4:8. How does this relate to Ps 24?

Pray

Begin by delighting in the Lord. Verbalize your love for Him and turn your heart towards Him. Ask Him to purify your heart and your motives. Ask Holy Spirit to reveal any area of your life mentioned in this Psalm that He wants to highlight or pour out His fire upon. Ask God to show you if there are behaviors or idols you are not aware of. Write down what He says to you. Close your time adoring the King of glory by telling Him who He is to you. Declare His attributes back to Him in worship. Delight in the fact that you are His and He is yours!

Connect

After prayerfully surrendering your heart to the Lord and listening to Holy Spirit, spend this time celebrating the King of Glory. Get outside if possible and revel in His creation, the work of His hands.

Celebrate the Mighty One who is about to come through you- His beloved!

Notes:

Day 10

Gazing on the Lord's Beauty

FROM THE HEAD...

Read: Psalm 27:4–8

Study

The presence of the Lord with His people was not just a theological fact to be discussed, or a reality to be celebrated (although it is those things). It was the deepest longing and yearning of the psalmist's heart in Ps 24:7: "One thing I ask of the Lord, this is what I seek: that I may dwell in the house of the Lord all the days of my life, to gaze upon the beauty of the Lord and to seek him in his temple." Like the other Psalms, the focal point of God's presence is the house of the Lord, where God met with His people. The most important thing to the Psalmist, the "one thing," was dwelling in the place God dwelled, seeking His face, and beholding the King's beauty. Because God met His people in the temple it was a place of refuge. The author of this Psalm, king David, finds refuge from his enemies and from danger in the secret place, where He encounters God. The presence of the Lord has become his stronghold, a safe place. In verse 5 David is confident that God will keep him safe if he draws near to God's presence. Therefore, God's people seek to dwell in the house of the Lord and seek Him in His temple as the 'one thing'.

There are a number of important phrases in verse 4. First, notice the repeated call to seek God's presence, to seek Him in His temple. In other words, the presence of God is something that God's people desire and wholeheartedly pursue. Second, it is interesting that while the sanctuary is God's dwelling place, His people are to "dwell" with Him in His temple. We are invited guests in the house of the Lord, the dwelling of God. Lest we think this is an occasional outing, the Psalmist's desire is to dwell there all the days of his life. Third, the goal of dwelling in the house of the Lord and seeking His presence is to gaze on the Lord's beauty. The idea here is not only aesthetic, but to see and experience God's goodness and favor upon us. To summarize, the Psalmist's desire is to experience a profound encounter with God's presence in His temple. No wonder the author expresses the confidence that he does in the very next verse: "For in the day of trouble He will keep me safe in his dwelling; He will hide me in the shelter of his sacred tent and set me high upon a rock" (v. 5). Psalm 91 reminds us of the same refuge in God's presence: "The one who dwells in the shelter of the Most High will rest in the shadow of the Almighty. I will say of the Lord, 'He is my refuge and my fortress'" (91:1–2).

When God's people seek to dwell in the sanctuary of God's presence, when they seek His face, God's presence becomes a refuge from the troubles of life. Likewise, the trouble that life brings our way should drive us into the refuge of the secret place of God's presence. When we do so we are able to rise above our circumstances, to be exalted above that which threatens us. The only response to God's presence is to sacrifice with songs of praise and worship found in verse 6. God's presence is a shelter that God's people run to in times of trouble. Encountering God's presence is the one thing! It should be the deepest longing of our hearts. Nothing else satisfies.

...TO THE HEART
Meditate

Psalm 27 is a cornerstone Psalm identifying the heart and pursuit of David which gives a contextual understanding of the Psalms and the heart from which they were written. Scholars believe this Psalm was written by David while in exile, possibly while in a cave running for his life from Saul or Absalom. Given this context, what was David's focus? Typically, crisis leads to survival mode solely focused on our own resources. How did David respond to his crisis? What was his gaze set upon? What would it look like to cultivate this precedence in your own life? Does your heart seek after this one thing to the degree expressed in this Psalm?

Pray

Take 30 minutes where you will be undistracted and undisturbed. Begin by turning the affections of your heart to Jesus. Recall what He has done for you. Tell Him your love for Him and communicate your desire for a greater capacity to hunger and to abide in his presence. Don't limit your time. Linger here and verbalize your prayer out loud, remembering that you are also speaking over your soul at this time as well! After a few minutes of directing your soul and mind in adoration of Him, spend the rest of your time sitting in silence before the Lord.

Connect

The key to this passage is found in the last verse, Ps 27:14, "WAIT." The Hebrew word for "wait" suggests that we entwine our soul with His. This is an active waiting, with expectation, an interweaving of your soul with His. Waiting can sometimes be a lengthy process; it is not bound by time. Sit and wait on the Lord, and stay until you hear his voice. Then stay longer. Listen and wait in expectation that He will speak. Entwine yourself with Him!

Notes:

Day 11

Desiring God

FROM THE HEAD...

Read: Psalm 84

Study

By now you should be convinced that God's presence with His people is a major theme in the Psalms. Psalm 84 is a prayer of longing and desire for the house of the Lord, the place which houses the presence of God. The Psalmist here expresses the intense desire to be with God, but also the joyful delight of experiencing God's presence. As you read the first couple of verses, notice how the writer describes his emotions when he thinks about God's dwelling place: "Lovely", "my soul yearns", it "faints", "my flesh and heart cry out". These are words of intense emotion and longing. The reason for this expression of emotion is that in the house of the Lord the people encounter the Almighty, the Living Lord Himself. It is not just about entering a physical structure, but engaging with the living Lord who dwells there.

Reflecting on the Lord's presence was an intense emotional experience for the writer, and it should be for us as well. The presence of God was not just a theological construct to be discussed. It was a reality to be pursued. It not only engages the mind, it excites desires and emotions. The psalmist pursued and desired God's dwelling place above everything else, and it brought unmatched joy and delight. There is blessing for those who dwell in the Lord's house; the response to God's presence is praise and worship. So important is God's presence, and so intense is the writer's desire for it, that everything and anything else pales in comparison. Therefore, the psalmist concludes that 'one day' in the courts of God's temple is better than 'one thousand days' anywhere else in the world. Think of the place you would rather be than anywhere else: Home with family, on a hiking trail, in the mountains, on a lake, or at a park. One day in God's courts (not even in the Holy of Holies!) is one thousand times better than any of these other places, as good and enjoyable as they are. The most amazing place you could possibly think of pales in comparison to time spent in God's presence. Therefore, it is to be desired above everything else. Even being a doorkeeper in the house of the Lord far exceeds any pleasure or joy in dwelling in the tents of the wicked. That is, even the most humble servant in God's temple, a mere doorkeeper, is far more desirable than any status the world and its pleasures offer. Absolutely nothing compares to spending time with the Lord. All other things recede into the background when making God's presence our ultimate goal and desire.

Those that seek intensely after God's presence find He is a shield who gives protection and a Lord who showers favor and good things on His people. God's presence is something to be intensely desired and pursued at all costs. Experiencing God's presence is far greater, far more important, and far more valuable than anything in this life we can experience or acquire.

...TO THE HEART
Meditate

This chapter sets expectations for what we should experience and gives perspective on what our yearning produces. First, let's identify what our expectation should be when engaging God's presence.

Secondly, let's discover through this passage how God has created our brain to cultivate an experiential knowledge of Him. Begin by reading the entire Psalm. Take note of the author's expectations and feelings when encountering the Living God. Write down how often the author expresses emotion or feeling. Next, write down verse 2. Look up the Hebrew definitions of soul, heart and flesh used in this verse and write down each definition. Now, read Matt 22:37. Look up the Greek definitions of heart, soul and mind. How do they correlate? What does the term 'cry out' imply? What does this mean for you?

Pray

Read through Ps 84 slowly and pray it to the Lord in the first person. Engage your heart. If you lack emotional connection with God, tell Him. Ask Him to awaken your spirit, to increase your hunger. Ask God to engage your heart, your mind, and your emotions with Him. Cry out to Him and allow the longing of your soul to find its home in Him.

Connect

We hunger after what we set our appetites upon. What we think about grows, as do our appetites towards wherever we direct them. Just as a man thinks in his heart, so is he (Prov 23:7). If we focus on stressful situations, or fear-based outcomes, we are strengthening that neural pathway in our brain. Alternatively, if we focus on the majesty of God, our identity in Christ, or our reality of abiding in God's presence, that reality will equally grow by creating and strengthening these neural pathways. Verse 5 states, "Blessed are those whose strength is in you, in whose heart are the highways to Zion."

God created our brains with the ability to form pathways of thought that become strengthened into 'highways' with repetitive thinking, called neuroplasticity.

We think first, and feelings follow. This neurological effect offers hope to anyone desiring more of the Lord. Create and strengthen your own neural pathways by writing down Biblical truths and speaking them over your mind, heart, will, and emotions. Declare God's goodness over yourself. Declare His character over you and your identity in Him. With these highways enroute, you too will find deep wells in the wilderness and pools of bliss when walking through the valley of tears. This is what living from His presence looks like!

Notes:

Day 12

Ascending into God's Presence

FROM THE HEAD...

Read: Psalms 120–135

Study

This portion of Psalms contains what are known as the Psalms of Ascents. It is typically Pss 120–134, however, we included Ps 135 in this portion as well. The Hebrew term for ascent is "going up". Some Old Testament scholars believed these fifteen psalms were sung as worshipers ascended the fifteen steps leading up to the temple in Jerusalem. Reading these passages in the context of pilgrimage into the Holy of Holies, or the secret place, gives insight into how to ascend, what to expect, and why.

Psalm 120

"In my distress I cried to the Lord". The Psalm opens with distress and the Psalmist pleading for relief from his accusers and enemies. This is his reality in that moment as his eyes are focused on the problems surrounding him. This could be categorized as the outer court of the Temple, representing the flesh, from our previous Temple analogy. Prayers from the flesh are often from a place of 'woe is me' and focus on self and negative circumstances. There isn't anything wrong with this- God wants us to come to Him, there is no right or wrong way to pray. This simply highlights the progression our prayers take as we get closer and closer to spirit to spirit communing with God in the secret place.

Psalm 121

"I will lift up my eyes to the hills, where my help comes from". The Psalmist begins by lifting his eyes to the Lord. His focus is shifting from circumstances to God. The transition from flesh to soul realm is taking place as the Psalmist remembers who God is and what God has done for him personally.

Psalm 122

"I was glad when they said, let us go into the house of the Lord". The focus in this psalm shifts outward. The 'I', 'me', and 'my' verbiage transitions to 'we', 'us', and 'our'. The Psalmist is speaking of worshipers in God's house, in terms of his brothers and companions, praying for peace of Jerusalem. His soul has been lifted after focusing on who God is and what God has done to a state of joy with an external focus, interceding for others.

Psalm 123

"Unto You I lift up my eyes, You who live in the heavens". The Psalmist is crying out to God for mercy. His eyes are on the Lord, and the language is that of a servant to a loving Master. The transition from soul to spirit is beginning.

Psalm 124

"If the Lord had not been on our side". This marks the transition from soul to spirit, or moving from the outer courts to the inner courts, as David continues to remember what God has done. However, this praise carries a slightly different tone than previous praise in 121. This praise is recalling and reminding his soul of the attributes of God versus what God did for him personally. Focus is corporate rather than singular on the nature and character of God.

Psalm 125- Psalm 126

"Those who trust in the Lord are like Mt Zion. It cannot be moved, it abides forever."

"When the Lord restored the captives of Zion, we were like those who dreamed."

Transition is taking place from soul to spirit, expressing total trust in the Lord and filled with hope by remembering what God has done in the past.

...TO THE HEART
Meditate

If we viewed each Psalm with a theme, we see the following progression of a similar path offered through the tabernacle imagery. There is no right or wrong way to encounter God, this simply highlights a progression which can occur in an hour, a season, or even a lifetime. In Ps 120, we first see one stepping into the outer courts, in the flesh, and the prayer offered from such a state. This moves into the Psalmist lifting their eyes to God, off their current circumstances. This results in his perspective turning from self to corporate. His gaze is on the Lord and is captivated by Him resulting in praise and thanksgiving for who God is. This Psalm is likened to stepping into the inner courts, from flesh to soul. Hope and joy fill their soul, while remembering what God has done and who He is The Psalmist expresses his trust in God resulting in surrender. This leads to purification and consecration, with a heart postured in humility. The next step of this progression leads into the Holy of Holies, or into the spirit realm. The Psalmist soul is quieted, his spirit is alive and overflowing in a state of bliss and delight in the love of the God.

Pray

Read through the Psalms, find one that resonates with you and begin to pray that prayer to the Lord as your own. Add your own personalization to it. Below are highlights from each of the portions of Scripture for today's passage you can use to walk through the progression into the Holy of Holies.

Connect

Connect your heart with God's presence through the above prayer. Stay in this place throughout the day. Use these prayers to recall your mind to engage with your spirit.

Notes:

Day 13

Ascending Into God's Presence

FROM THE HEAD...

Read: Psalm 120–135

Study

Continuing through the Psalms, read through the portions below making your own notes as to the Psalmist progression into the Holy of Holies.

Psalm 127- Psalm 128

The focus of these Psalms is the blessings of God and fear of the Lord. The heart posture is one of recognizing God's blessings from a place of humility and obedience to the Lord. This is the place of surrender leading to adoration. The Psalmist's heart is alive with adoring praise as he speaks of the goodness that flows from God.

Psalm 129-Psalm 130

These Psalms lead into the inner courts, the Holy place, with a maturing love, one that trusts and praises in the midst of suffering. Both Ps 129 and 130 are of purification and cleansing, one through suffering and one through repentance. Before entering into the Holy of Holies we see the purification theme throughout Scripture. Psalm 130 speaks of a consecration, a plea and cry for mercy, however, this time it isn't to save from the enemy, but to save from sin. This is the catalyst into the realm of the spirit.

Psalm 131

This Psalm represents one entering into the Holy of Holies, the spirit has taken over. Humility marks the posture and the soul is quieted, at peace, likened to a weaned and happy baby perfectly content. Rest and quiet trust are the results of this stage of prayer, and all striving has ceased.

Psalm 132

This is the place where God lights upon your heart and implants His purposes and callings within you. Similar to the progression in Isa 6, there is purification, cleansing, humility and repentance followed by being 'sent out' with God's direct instructions. It was in God's Presence David's pursuit began to build God a resting place. This became his one obsession, and it came from the secret place.

Psalm 133–135

A by-product of being in the Holy of Holies is being filled to overflowing with love. Adoration for God, love for others and love for the house of God characterize the worshiper. An overwhelming sense of joy and delight floods every aspect of your being, with blessings and praises bursting forth.

...TO THE HEART
Meditate

Reread the "To the Heart" section from Day 12 again. Do you see the progression in these Psalms? Which Psalm do you identify with the most right now? Why do you think the Israelites sang songs as they ascended? Read carefully through these Psalms again and summarize in your own words the message of each one.

Pray

Continue the same exercise from yesterday. Choose a Psalm from today's reading that correlates with your heart today. Pray this to the Lord and personalize it with your own words to God. Progress through to engage your heart in intimacy with Him!

Connect

Maintain the heart of surrender with a mindset of consecration as you go about your daily tasks. Recall to mind God's spirit inside you and live from that place today.

Notes:

Day 14

Intimacy with God

FROM THE HEAD...

Read: Song of Songs 5

Study:

We now come to a book you might not think to associate with the theme of the presence of God in Scripture: The Song of Songs! At first glance it looks like it has nothing at all to do with it! It appears to be a book written by king Solomon, king David's son, celebrating the physical love between a husband and wife, as it is full of intimate language. Most likely, it was originally written to celebrate the intimate love between husband and wife, the "they will become one flesh" aspect of the marriage union from Gen 2:24. However, throughout history, both Jewish and Christian scholars have also seen this book as having an additional, deeper significance as a picture of God's intimate relationship with His people. Rather than choosing between the two approaches, it is probably a "both...and". In other words, we should probably read the Song of Songs on two levels: First, it celebrates the intimacy, the one flesh union, between a husband and wife at a human and physical level. But second, within the broader context of the entirety of Scripture, where God is portrayed in the Old Testament as a husband and Israel His wife (Isa 54:5-8; Jer 2:1-3; Ezek 23; Hos 1-3), and in the New Testament Jesus is the husband with the church His bride (Eph 5:21-33; Rev 19:7-9; 21:2, 9), we are also justified in reading the Song of Songs as a picture of the intimate relationship between God and us. Interestingly, the very next book after the Song of Songs is the book of Isaiah, which most often portrays the relationship between God and His people in marriage terms (49:18; 54:5-6; 61:10; 62:4-5).

In Eph 5:21-33, Paul explicitly sees the relationship between a husband and wife as a picture of the relationship between Christ and His church. In fact, Paul even quotes from Gen 2:24, that the two "will become one flesh", in verse 31, but he understands it as speaking of the mystery of Christ and His church (v. 32): The "one flesh" intimate union between husband and wife points to the deeper intimate union between Christ and His church. We should read the Song of Songs in the same manner. The "one flesh" intimacy between a husband and wife points to and illustrates an even deeper intimacy between God and His people. An ancient Jewish writing called the Targum (written in the Aramaic language) on the Song of Songs interpreted part of the Song as a reference to the temple which Solomon built. The cedars and pomegranates in Song of Songs indicated the temple, which God's presence dwelt. The intimacy celebrated in the Song of Songs is equivalent to the intimate encounter in the Holy of Holies. Therefore, the Song of Songs can be seen as a picture of the intimate encounter with God's presence He intends for His people individually to experience, an intimacy deeper and even more satisfying than any physical intimacy and pleasure at the human level.

To consider just one example, in chapter 5 of Song of Songs, the chapter you read, we encounter the language of beauty and fragrance (myrrh, spice, honey, dew), of desperate longing, single-hearted devotion and intense seeking, excited expectation, the language of incomparability and praise, all to describe the relationship between the husband and wife. There is excitement for encounter ("my heart began to pound for him", v. 4). The presence and love of the husband is desired above all else. He is incomparable, "outstanding among ten thousand" (v. 10). She is lovestruck for her lover. So desirous is she of his presence that she is distressed when he is absent (v. 6). How true this is with human relationships. But how much more so at the divine level with our relationship to God. God's people should be in love with their God; desiring His presence above all else; nothing and no one else comes close to comparing to Him; His beauty surpasses all else; there is excitement for encounter with Him and intense seeking; He is outstanding among ten thousand; we are grieved when we do not spend time with Him. We should long intensely for intimacy with their Beloved!

...TO THE HEART
Meditate

If viewing Song of Songs in this light seems a stretch, read The Passion Translation of this book. For centuries this book of the Bible has been linguistically interpreted as typical, dramatic, mythological, literal or allegorical. The Song could be read at more than one level, and The Passion Translation translated Song of Songs contextually in light of God's relationship with mankind. Before understanding the intimacy God invites us to experience in Song of Songs, we first must have a bedrock of foundational truths to build upon. If these bedrock truths are not core beliefs, one will miss entirely the passionate call of God's intimate nature of His heart towards us. The first foundational truth is believing and knowing God speaks to you personally.

The second foundational key is believing He wants *you* to possess an experiential knowledge of His personal love and delight. Delight opens the door. Religion has taught us to keep God at a distance through formality and ritual. Relationship draws us near. As long as God is distant and uninvolved with personal affairs, we tend to live as orphans stuck in sin cycles rather than His beloved child and bride exercising our inherited authority. Religion tells us God is not available, that He is not interested in personal intimate relationship, He doesn't speak to us personally, and it is unbiblical to expect to hear His voice or experience Him through delight. If any of these beliefs have permeated your heart, write them down. Confess these to the Lord and ask for Scriptural truths to replace them. Song 1:2 instructs one how to begin. Allow Him to smother you with His love, just as a husband is so enamored with his wife. Allow God to cover your heart with His love. Your role is to surrender and yield. Allow God to awaken you with the kisses of His Word to your heart. Rest in God's passionate love towards you, He is coming to awaken and draw you away into His love!

Pray

Ask Holy Spirit to come and awaken your heart as you read Song of Songs. Surrender self-protective armor or defenses as you come before Him. Pray that the very source and root of your life would be found in the resting place of His love for you. Pray that He would unveil your understanding so you would be able to discover the magnitude of Christ's personal love towards you. Ask that He would fill you to overflowing with His love, beyond measure and comprehension. Thank Him and express your love and adoration for Him.

Connect

Anticipation marks the tone of Song of Songs, anticipation of hearing the voice of your Beloved, expectancy knowing He is there to speak with you. This mindset is the hallmark of the relationship between God and us. Believe Jesus is waiting to meet with you, that you will hear from Him for today and experience His wrap-around love. This is the key to engaging His heart! Challenge yourself to rise early, before dawn, and watch the sunrise with Jesus. Drive someplace to be alone as He awakens your heart in awe as you watch the first wonder of the day in the glory of His creation. Read Song 2:8–15 as if Jesus is speaking to you. Allow Him to fill you with His love for you and let Him encounter you in the deep places of your heart. Expect Him to meet with you; anticipate His voice!

Notes:

Day 15

A Glimpse of God's Holiness

FROM THE HEAD...

Read: Isaiah 6:1–8

Study

While God's earthly dwelling is in His tabernacle and temple in the midst of the people, His true dwelling is in heaven. The earthly temple is only a reflection of the true, heavenly temple above. The prophet Isaiah is privileged to enter the heavenly throne room and dwelling place of God, the place of His glorious presence, in chapter 6. Isaiah is not just getting a glimpse into heaven, but into the heavenly *temple*. When Isaiah describes what he saw he tells us that the robe of God filled the "temple" (v. 1). In heaven's throne room God is surrounded by angelic beings, the Seraphim. These may be represented by the angels that guarded the Garden of Eden when Adam and Eve were expelled, and the cherubim that guarded the ark of the covenant in the Holy of Holies. Now they guard the presence of God in the heavenly temple. The Seraphim's (winged angelic beings) job is also to worship God before the throne. The song they sing in verse 3 is "Holy, holy, holy is the Lord Almighty." God is holy and separate from everything and everyone else. But

His intention is to one day fill the entire earth with His glory: "The whole earth is full of His glory."

The throne room is even filled with smoke at one point, just as the Holy of Holies was in the tabernacle and temple. Notice the two effects that encountering God's presence has on the prophet Isaiah. First, God's presence revealed Isaiah's sinfulness with a purifying effect. When Isaiah stands in the presence of a Holy God he cries out, "Woe to me. I am ruined! For I am a man of unclean lips, and I live among a people of unclean lips, and my eyes have seen the King, the Lord Almighty" (v. 5). God sends one of the Seraphim to Isaiah with a hot coal from the heavenly altar, touches his lips with it, and atones for his sin. Isaiah is purified, and God restored his identity. God requires holiness and purity of anyone who would stand in His presence to encounter Him (Pss 15, 24). He cannot dwell with sin. Yet it is God's presence that purifies and transforms us so that we are worthy to stand in His presence!

The second thing that happens to Isaiah in God's presence is a commission for service. Encountering God's presence results in a fresh assignment and commissioning to serve the Lord. It is not enough for His people to simply experience and enjoy His presence. Rather, it issues a call to service and obedience: "Then I heard the voice of the Lord saying, 'Whom shall I send? And who will go for us?' And I said, 'Here am I. Send me'" (v. 8). God's presence not only exposes sin and purifies His people, but commissions them for service to be sent out as His representatives.

...TO THE HEART
Meditate

Isaiah 6 is an account of a very real place, the heavenly throne room. This was not a figment of Isaiah's imagination or an ethereal vision. It exists right now, with activity this very moment. It is a tangible place in existence regardless of distance or whether you have seen it with your physical eye. There are angelic beings who are singing 'Holy, holy, holy' to the Lord this very minute. Allowing this reality to overcome our reality is foundational in stepping into greater realms of intimacy. Based on this passage, write down a description of the throne room from Isa 6, as if you were writing to someone a description of a place you visited. Ask questions of this passage. What does high and lifted up mean? Why does God's robe fill the temple, and what does that mean? Why are the Seraphim covering their faces and feet? What is significant about that? What does it mean that the whole earth is filled with His glory? Is that right now or later? What does that look like practically and what is your role in that? Why did the progression of this chapter occur in the timeline it did?

Ask the five W's, who-what-when-where-why of each line, thought, concept and detail. Allot time to listen to Holy Spirit as He reveals the Word and brings it to life. Every word is living and active, written for you to profit, to be taught, reproved, trained, and equipped! Let's dive in!

Pray

After meditating on this passage, spend time in prayerful worship. Take communion and come boldly before the throne of grace. Spend time worshiping. Linger in His presence.

Connect

Think about this vision of the throne room again. Did Isaiah leave the throne room the same? What changed? How does this reality impact you personally with your time in God's presence?

Notes:

Day 16

Vision of a Future Temple

FROM THE HEAD...

Read: Ezekiel 43:1-5

Study

In Ezek 40-48 the prophet has a vision of a new, heavenly temple that is to be established one day in the future. Remember, Israel has been taken away into exile by a foreign nation, Babylon, because of their idolatry and unfaithfulness to God. God cannot make His home in the presence of sin. In Ezek 8-11, the prophet sees God's glory depart from Jerusalem and the temple. The picture is tragic. The temple is still standing but is vacant of God's presence. However, in chapters 40-48, Ezekiel foresees a day when God will once again establish a dwelling place among his people. His glory will return to live in a new temple and they will encounter God's glorious presence again! In fact, the Presence of the Lord may be the dominant theme of the entire book of Ezekiel!

The first three chapters, 40-42, describe the temple and its dimensions as the prophet is given a guided tour of the future temple. It is a glorious building that far exceeds anything Israel had seen before. Like the previous temple, it consisted of an outer court, a Holy Place, and then the Holy of Holies, the special place

Vision of a Future Temple

of God's intimate presence. Ezekiel describes the walls and gates with detailed measurements. The act of measuring shows completion and perfection: This is the complete and perfect dwelling place of God. It also shows protection and preservation. God's dwelling is protected from evil, sin, and enemies, as are His people who reside there. But the high point of the vision is when God's presence comes to fill it in 43:1–4: "And I saw the glory of the God of Israel coming from the east. His voice was like the roar of rushing waters, and the land was radiant with His glory. . . . The glory of the Lord entered the temple through the gate facing east." Until this point the temple is apparently empty. But now it is full. The glory that left the temple in chapter 8, has now returned to it. God Himself speaks to the significance: "This is where I will live among the Israelites forever" (v. 7), and "I will live among them forever" (v. 9). God's glory clearly refers to God's very presence. It is interesting that His glory enters from the East. The east was significant as it was the direction the sun rose. It signifies a new beginning, new life, and darkness into light. God's presence brings newness, life, illumination, and joy. East was also the direction of entry into the Garden of Eden, the entrance guarded by two angels after Adam and Eve were removed because of sin (Gen 3:24). Now God's glorious presence enters through the east gate of the future temple.

Since the Garden of Eden, God's intention has been to dwell with mankind, to manifest His presence among us, and for us to encounter Him. This was why God commanded His people to build a tabernacle and temple. Though He removed His presence from their midst due to sin, God's intention to live among His people would not be thwarted. God once more manifests His brilliant presence to be available to man forever. Ezekiel 48 ends with an anticipation that God's presence would burst the bounds of the temple: The name of the city is "The Lord is There" (48:35). The entire city would be a place of God's presence, all would have access to it. This anticipates what we will find more fully in the New Testament, Christ makes unhindered access possible to the very presence of God for all people at all times.

...TO THE HEART
Meditate

This passage is pregnant with the reality we get to walk in today, beholding the glory of the Lord with His presence becoming the place of our abiding. There are two themes in this passage: Purification and consecration unto honoring God's name, and keeping His ordinances resulting in the glory of the Lord filling His temple. Within these themes, what is the appropriation of this Old Testament passage for us today? Where is God's temple today? Where does He abide? What gets filled with His glory today? Read 2 Cor 6:16 and 1 Cor 6:19. What is the context of both of these passages? Why is purification and consecration so important to the Lord?

Pray

Take a few minutes to sit before Jesus and offer Him your heart. See God on His throne in your heart. If anything comes to mind hindering you from engaging with God, quickly repent and ask Jesus to cleanse you. Yield every area of your life again to His Lordship. Using the Word of God as your guide, read Ps 63 over yourself. Turn your gaze to Jesus, turn your spirit inward to Christ who dwells within you, and engage your spirit with His. God promises to take us from glory to glory, a continual filling. Yield to His Spirit within you, and see yourself walking in the newness of life, being filled with His glory!

Connect

God is jealous over us and our hearts. He aims to protect us from separation from Him and the voice of the accuser by giving specifics on how to live in holiness with fullness of joy and freedom! Each time we come before Him, view it as a call to purification and to realign your priorities for honoring the temple of the Lord. God is holy and requires holiness of those who seek His face. Jesus is our righteousness, and we cannot attempt this on our own. It comes from Jesus who makes us holy when we live and walk in the Spirit. Consecration is a natural response to His holiness and overwhelming love. When we see His face, we want nothing less. We can engage with God internally, communing with Him in our spirit while we go about our day (Col 1:27). Remember, there is always more for you- there is no capping of His glory or reaching the end of His love. Keep pressing in; there is so much more!

Notes:

Day 17

The Life-Giving Water of God's Presence

FROM THE HEAD...

Read: Ezekiel 47:1-12

Study

After Ezekiel is shown the future restored temple and God's glorious presence filling it in chapters 40-43, Ezekiel is then shown another feature of this future temple in chapter 47. At the entrance of the temple Ezekiel sees a stream of water flowing out under the threshold. When Ezekiel follows this flow outside, it becomes a river, which at first is only ankle-deep. As he walks a little further it becomes knee-deep, then a little further waist-deep, and finally it becomes too deep to cross. This flowing water is life-giving. It spreads life throughout the land, to living creatures, and to numerous trees which bear fruit. The fruit from the trees provides food and their leaves bring healing. Like the river in Ps 46 which makes glad the city of God, Ezekiel's river signifies life, abundance, and blessing that God gives to His people. This is the same river that will flow through the New Jerusalem in Rev 22:1-2. The fact that it comes from the temple in Ezekiel tells us it is the result of God's presence within us. God's presence brings life and abundance, shown by the metaphor of a river. This life and abundance is ever-increasing as it grows deeper and deeper, flowing from the temple. God's presence and blessing overwhelm us the more we experience it. It is inexhaustible. We cannot hope to plumb the depths of God's glorious presence within us. It is even able to turn a Dead Sea fresh, bringing life where there has only been death!

Both the river that flows from the temple and the fruit bearing trees are meant to recall the Garden of Eden. Remember that was the first temple on earth, the place God dwelled with His people. There was a river that watered the Garden of Eden (Gen 2:10–14). There were trees for fruit in the Garden, and the Tree of Life (2:9). The Garden of Eden was a temple, a sanctuary where God manifested His presence. What is this suggesting? Ezekiel's temple is to be seen as God restoring His presence that was originally accessible in the Garden of Eden but lost because of sin. Paradise lost is now paradise gained! God's presence encountered in the Garden of Eden is now available in Ezekiel's restored temple. That is, the temple is the fulfillment of God's intention for His people in the Garden. God does not shift course of action, or resort to plan B. He desires an intimate relationship with His people.

Do you see the pattern? God dwelled in the garden, but Adam and Eve were removed from God's presence because of sin. Then God established His tabernacle and temple, but Israel was removed from God's presence because of sin. But God is not finished. He will once again restore His dwelling place so we can encounter Him intimately. As a result, anyone dwelling in His presence lives in fullness of life, abundance, joy, and healing in inexhaustible supply. The river that Ezekiel sees in his vision anticipates the life Jesus will give through the outpouring of the Holy Spirit (see John 7:37–38). In the broader context of Scripture, the river of water is the Holy Spirit. We experience this unending life in God's presence when we drink of the living water of the Holy Spirit. God wants His presence to be our constant supply to flow over us, engulf us, and flow through us.

The Life-Giving Water of God's Presence

...TO THE HEART

Meditate

Read John 7:37–38. Meditate on what it practically looks like to be filled with Holy Spirit so He is constantly flowing out of you. Where would you say you are standing now if you were in Ezekiel's vision? Ankle deep, waist deep, or caught up in the current? What part of your life do you need the fullness of God's presence to fill with His abundance, joy and healing? What is keeping you from going deeper in, or what is keeping His presence from overflowing the banks in every aspect of your life?

Pray

Begin by focusing your heart and mind on loving Jesus. Connect your heart with His overwhelming love for you. Give God praise and specific thanks for who He is to you. Ask Holy Spirit to come and fill you. Tell Him you want to experience more and you long to go deeper. Ask Holy Spirit for His grace to empower you to fully experience God's glory. Pray Eph 3:14–20 in the first person.

Connect

Imagine the Holy Spirit as a river washing over you and filling you, every nook and cranny of your life. If He was a river gushing out of you, what daily activities would be affected? What would you expect? Build your faith and expectation, dream with Holy Spirit for your life.

Notes:

Day 18

Making God's Presence a Priority

FROM THE HEAD...

Read: Malachi 1

Study

The prophet Haggai was commissioned by the Lord to prophesy to the Israelites after they returned home from exile. Israel had gone into bondage under a foreign country, Babylon, because of their disobedience to God and the Law He gave them. After a period of discipline God has allowed His people to return to their land. Another people, the Persians, conquered the Babylonians who held Israel captive, and the Persian ruler, Cyrus, allowed Israel to return to the land they once occupied. However, all is not well in the land God gave back to them. There is no temple, no place to encounter and worship God. The temple had been destroyed by the Babylonians when the Israelites were taken into captivity. They have returned to their homeland and it still lies in ruins.

The prophet Haggai, speaking the words of the Lord, begins with the problem: "The people say, 'The time has not yet come for the Lord's house to be built'" (1:2). The problem is far more than just neglecting the restoration of a building. This building is nothing less than the very dwelling place of God, the place where they can experience intimate encounters with God's presence. The temple should be the center of their life and worship, and they seem to think they can somehow survive without it. All the while, they live in nice, paneled houses (v. 4). Paneled houses were fit for kings! The people lived like royalty, yet God's house was ignored and still laid in ruins. God's house, the temple, and therefore God's presence, was not a priority to the people. Their own agendas took priority over the dwelling place of God. The prophet Haggai tells the people in verses 5-6 to think about something else: This lack of priority to the dwelling of God is why they are struggling and not seeing God's blessing. Their planting yields a subpar harvest. They are still hungry after eating and thirsty after drinking, because they don't have enough food and drink. Their clothes don't keep them warm, they never have enough money. Drought has affected crops, cattle, and livelihood (1:10-11). In other words, no matter what they tried and how hard they worked, it all fell to the ground. This was the result of not making God's presence a priority by allowing the temple to remain in ruins. Little wonder they were not experiencing God's blessings.

In order to reverse this, God commands His people to go cut down timber in the mountains to build the temple (1:7-8). Verses 12-15 records how the people obeyed God and began to rebuild His house, making God's presence a priority again. The key is they heard God's voice and obeyed. Obedience brings blessing. Because of sin, they were a defiled people; however, with a rebuilt temple, they would experience God's renewed blessing (2:10-19). Remember, this is more than just construction of a nice building - it is an act of obedience that prioritizes God's presence.

Notice another important theme occurring in this brief book. Five times the people are commanded by the Lord to "Give careful thought" (1:5, 7, 2:15, 18 [2 times]). God's presence is to be taken seriously; it requires careful consideration. There are consequences of missing blessings due to neglect of His presence. God's presence cannot be taken lightly. Haggai reminds us of the seriousness of making God's dwelling in us a priority and the blessing that comes from prioritizing times of worship and seeking His presence in our lives.

...TO THE HEART
Meditate

What does Malachi imply about priorities? What value does God place on worship and its priority? If this was to become your first priority, what would it require of you? What would it look like to "Give careful thought" to making God's presence your priority? He began with a call to reassess priorities with warnings of consequences and ends with a promise and exhortation. In essence, He asks, "Who among you remembers when your heart was rightly aligned, when I consumed you, when your first love of Me dictated your life?" He asks now, "In comparison, does it not matter to you?" If your heart is stirred once again, take heart. "Be strong and work towards this" says the Lord, for He is with you. Meditate on His promise He gives at the end of the chapter: That the place of encounter they were building will be even *greater* than what they formerly encountered. Imagine what this greater measure of glory could look like in your own life!

Pray

Sit with Holy Spirit and ask Him for practical specifics on the questions below:

Do I place the same value on engaging with God and worshiping Him throughout the day as He does? Is hosting His presence the center of my life? What needs to change for it to be so?

Connect

Being His temple requires daily whole-hearted surrender, placing Jesus as the most desirable of your affections, obedience to His voice in the smallest details, and daily consecration. Recall when your heart was rightly aligned, when God consumed you, when your first love of Jesus dictated your life. Ask God to stir your heart once again, to awaken hunger within you. Commit the rearranging of your priorities to the Lord and thank Him for His glory that is coming for you!

Notes:

Day 19

God With Us

FROM THE HEAD...

Read: Matthew 1:23

Study

When we get to the New Testament a major shift takes place in how God's presence is mediated to His people. In the Old Testament the tabernacle and temple played a key role in the mediation of God's presence. However, now, the presence of God is no longer restricted to the tabernacle, temple, or even a specific city (Jerusalem). God's presence will be mediated through a *person*, Jesus Christ. The presence and glory of God that dwelled in the tabernacle and temple will now be accessible in relationship to the person of Christ. The glorious presence of God dwelling in Christ is what the tabernacle and temple were foreshadowing and pointing to. This also means there is no differentiation of those who can access God's presence: All people, not just high priests or Israelites, will now have equal access to the gift of God's presence.

In Matthew's account of the Christmas story, Mary is found to be pregnant, and Joseph, not realizing this is a supernatural conception through the power of the Holy Spirit, determines to break off the betrothal (similar to our engagement, but not exactly), most likely suspecting she has been unfaithful to him. God sends an angel to Joseph to tell him the news this baby is not the result of normal human means of conception, but from the Holy Spirit, and that he should take Mary as his wife. The verse I want to focus on is verse 23. Matthew tells us the birth of Jesus by a young virgin is nothing less than the fulfillment of Old Testament Scriptures. This baby Mary would give birth to would be called 'Emmanuel' in fulfillment of Isa 7:14. In our day names don't always carry great significance—sometimes they have a family history, we just like the name, or maybe we want to be original. But during the time of Christ, names carried great significance. In fulfillment of Isa 7:14, Matthew insists the child is going to be called Emmanuel, and this is for a reason. The name Emmanuel is actually interpreted for us by Matthew himself: It means "God is with us" - *Emmanu* = with us; *El* = God. God could not be any clearer as to the significance of this birth: With the birth of Jesus, God is present *with His people*.

That phrase "God with us" has deeper Old Testament significance. God promised to be "with" Abraham. He was with Abraham's family, and with the nation of Israel that would come from Abraham. He was "with Moses". He was "with" the Israelites through the desert and into the promised land. He was "with" David. He was "with" His people in the temple. Now it is in the person of Jesus Christ, God is *with* His people in a more personal way. This theme of God's presence with us through the person of Jesus will get picked up in other New Testament books, as well. The significance here is with the birth of Christ in Bethlehem, God's promises to be "with" His people climaxes through God's presence in Jesus. With the coming of Christ to earth, God is "with us" apart from a tabernacle, temple, a specific city, or a specific people.

The book of Matthew ends with another reminder of God's presence with His people through Jesus. At the end of the Gospel, Jesus commissions His disciples to make disciples of all the nations. He promises His presence with them: "I am *with you* until the end of the age" (28:20). The theme of divine presence acts like "bookends" to the entire book of Matthew, showing this is the dominant theme of the book. God is present with His people through Jesus, starting with His birth and continuing through their mission into eternity. This promise of God's presence through Jesus provides encouragement and enablement for worldwide mission.

...TO THE HEART
Meditate

God with us! God IN us. That concept alone seems too much for our finite minds to grasp. Though this is our reality in position, how often do we live this experientially? What keeps us from living and dwelling moment-by-moment in the reality that the same One who raised Jesus from the dead, God Himself, dwells inside us? The only thing that keeps us from experiencing the reality of this magnificent miracle of God indwelling us is ourselves. Our thoughts and beliefs often determine what we experience, in terms of whether we allow limiting beliefs or we allow truth to renew our minds. 2 Corinthians 10:4–5 tells us to "Take every thought captive and demolish every stronghold that comes against the knowledge of God." This doesn't happen just once; it's a daily activity. Acknowledging and addressing fears or hindrances is the first step in overcoming strongholds of thinking that limit us from experiencing the fullness of God. Read today's passage and meditate on God with you as Emmanuel. Write down the significance of this in light of your daily schedule. How would this change each aspect of your day?

Pray

Ask Holy Spirit to bring to mind any limiting beliefs or offenses you have about God, or yourself, that inhibit the reality of God's indwelling presence. If any are revealed, ask Him to show you Scriptural passages that refute that belief. Spend time worshiping Jesus and the fact He is *with* you, *in* you and *for* you. Soak in His presence!

Connect

Take the Scripture verses Holy Spirit gave you and write them down. Declare these over your soul. Make these a part of your daily declarations of God's truth over yourself. An example of this would be:

> "I am the temple of the Holy Spirit. The same Spirit that raised Jesus from the dead lives in me. I carry the fullness of Christ within me. It is God's good pleasure to pour out His Spirit and His glory over my house, my family, my church, and my city. I yield myself wholly and fully to the Lordship of Christ as I walk obediently and faithfully. I expect His glory to cover and to fill me to overflowing in every area of my life, including my relationships, my choices, my past, and my future. I am my Beloved's and He is mine."

Notes:

Day 20

Occupied 'with' Christ vs. Occupied 'for' Christ

FROM THE HEAD...

Read: Luke 10:38-42

Study

In one of the more well-known stories about Jesus in the Gospels we learn an important lesson about prioritizing time spent in the presence of God. We have already noticed an important shift has taken place in the New Testament. No longer is the presence of God limited to a physical structure, the tabernacle and temple. No longer is access to the presence of God restricted to specific people, Israel, or groups, such as priests. Now God's presence is found in the person of God's Son, Jesus. He is the place where God's glorious presence resides. He is Immanuel, God with us! Now it is through Christ we encounter God's presence intimately. Jesus teaches an important lesson about prioritizing God's presence in Luke 10:38-42. In His travels Jesus visits a village, which we know from John 12:1-3 was the town of Bethany, where Mary and Martha lived. When Jesus arrived in the village, Martha and Mary opened their home to Him.

The respective responses of these two women to Jesus when he arrives is most important in this story. We see that when Jesus entered their home, Mary sat at Jesus' feet and listened attentively to Him, probably to His teaching. But, we see that Martha was distracted with all the preparations for Jesus' visit, such as preparing the meal. Naturally, Martha responds by wondering why Jesus doesn't seem to care she is doing all the work and preparation, while Mary doesn't help, but simply sits and listens to Jesus. She implores Jesus: "Tell her to help me!" Jesus' words in verses 41–42 respond to Martha's request, but also provide Jesus' evaluation of the two women's actions towards Him. Jesus' response, and whom He sides with, is probably unexpected for most readers of this story. Basically, he approved of and sides with Mary, who simply sat and listened to Jesus. He does not say Martha is wrong in what she did or her response. This was a natural and expected response: To show hospitality to a guest, especially Jesus. But He characterizes Martha's actions as that of agitation and worry. She forgot the main point was not to be busy for the guest but to spend time with the guest! One would think Martha would get the highest praise—she is busying herself serving Jesus, the son of God and Messiah. Yet Jesus praises Mary instead, for she has chosen the better thing, to sit and listen to Jesus, to be preoccupied with Him. Her focus is on Jesus, spending time in His presence.

The message of this short story is the importance of being preoccupied with Christ rather than to be busy for Him. It is far more important to spend time in God's presence, listening to His voice, than to be endlessly busy while accomplishing things for Him, especially under our own strength. However, Jesus is not saying we should never accomplish things for Him, nor be active in service. These verses are not a free pass from engaging the world. The Gospels are filled with calls to be active in serving the Lord, helping the poor, and healing the sick. However, being busy for the Lord is not a substitute for spending time with the Lord, sitting before Him, being still and listening to His voice. Service for and to Christ flows out of spending time with Christ. Performing acts of service in our own strength results in busyness and worry. Our obedience, service, and ministry should stem from intimacy with Christ, sitting in His presence and listening to His voice.

...TO THE HEART
Meditate

God's Presence is a choice. It is a daily choice to sit at His feet, to hunger after His voice above all others, to gaze upon His beauty. God doesn't make this choice for us; in fact, we are directed to ask God for it (Ps 27) and urged to seek His face. Yet, the choice to respond is ours. How we respond will determine the dimension of intimacy we experience. In the passage of Mary and Martha, in Luke 10, they both love Jesus, they both minister to Him and are both in the presence of Jesus, but only one was hungry for His presence. The difference between Mary and Martha wasn't choice of activity, but one of priorities. Mary chose the One thing, to posture her heart to gaze at Jesus despite what it looked like, or who was offended by it. Martha was getting caught up in the act of serving Jesus while not connecting with His heart in the secret place, which led to comparison and competition. What other characteristics mark Martha? What takes precedence in your life over intimacy with Jesus? How do you know when tasks begin to overtake your hunger for Him?

Pray

Set aside at least an hour, or even more, to worship Jesus. No phone, no TV, just simple undistracted devotion from an undivided heart. Allow your heart to receive His love and saturate your soul with His words to you and over you! Be sure to spend ample time listening to Him!

Connect

Intimacy with God positions you as a friend and lover, no longer just a servant. This is the posture of a bride. Hunger for His presence can be chosen. God initiates our hunger, and we get to respond by seeking after Him. Ask the Lord now to increase your hunger so you can become a bride abandoned to your bridegroom.

Notes:

Day 21

Beholding God's Glory in Jesus

FROM THE HEAD...

Read: John 1:14, 18

Study

John 1:1–18 has often been called the Prologue to John's Gospel. In it we find major themes that will be developed in the rest of the Gospel. It primarily tells us who Jesus is and what He came to accomplish as the One sent by God from heaven to earth. It introduces us to the Jesus we read about in the rest of the Gospel. In John 1 we are introduced to Jesus as the Word (*Logos*). Jesus is the very speech, the communication, and the discourse of God. Jesus comes to reveal God to us, to speak God's truth to us. This Word not only preexisted with God, but is identified as God Himself (1:1).

This Word who was with God and is God, in verse 14 takes on human nature and a physical body: "And the Word became flesh." This event is known by theologians as the *incarnation*, when God took on human flesh. Now, we often stop right here, but if you keep reading John tells us something else we shouldn't miss: "... and [the Word] *dwelled* among us, and we beheld His *glory*, the *glory* of the One and Only who came from the Father." Do you remember those two words "dwell" and "glory" from some of the Old Testament passages you have already read and studied? These two words, "dwell" and "glory", are used of God's presence in the tabernacle and temple in the Old Testament! Notice the words highlighted in the passages below. When God instructed Moses and Israel to build the tabernacle He said, "Then have them make a sanctuary for me, and I will dwell among them" (Exod 25:8). When the tabernacle was completed, we read: "Then the cloud covered the Tent of Meeting, and the glory of the Lord filled the tabernacle. Moses could not enter the tent of meeting because the cloud had settled upon it, and the glory of the Lord filled the tabernacle" (Exod 40:34–35). With the account of the building of the temple (a permanent tabernacle), we read: "When the priests withdrew from the Holy Place, the cloud filled the temple of the Lord. And the priests could not perform their service because of the cloud, for the glory of the Lord filled His temple. Then Solomon said, 'The Lord has said that he will dwell in a dark cloud. I have indeed built a magnificent temple for You, a place for You to dwell forever" (1 Kgs 8:10–13). So when we read in John that Jesus "dwelled among us" and "we beheld his glory" (John 1:14), we are hearing tabernacle and temple language!

The point: Jesus is the new and true tabernacle. *He* is now the place where God's glory will dwell, not in a physical structure. Verse 1 sets us up by stating the Word was God. If the Word, Jesus, is God, that is where God's presence will be found. The presence of God which resided in the tabernacle and temple in the Old Testament is now found only in the person of Christ. It is now in personal relationship with Jesus that we encounter the presence of God. When you move on to the last verse of the prologue (v. 18) we are reminded of another Old Testament concept: "No one has ever seen God." However, now we can see God because Jesus the Word, who was with God and is God, is the One who reveals the Glory of God. In Jesus, the invisible God becomes visible in the Word who has become human flesh. Jesus is the new and true temple of God. He now takes the place of the tabernacle and temple as He is the reality they pointed to. In Christ we now behold God's glorious presence. Intimate relationship with Jesus is how we enjoy access to encounter the living God.

...TO THE HEART
Meditate

This is going to be a time of soaking in His love, His word, and enjoying His presence. There are several verses below to springboard you into encountering Him. Remember, you are meeting with a person. He has thoughts and feelings and longs to spend time with you. He isn't deaf or mute. He speaks and He listens to every thought in your heart. He is within you, Christ in you, who is the hope of glory. Slowly read the passages below with an expectation to encounter Jesus word by word. The word is living and active. Jesus, the eternal Word is alive inside you. So engage your spirit as you actively encounter the Word of life through His words: Col 1:27, John 17:20-24

Pray

I invite you to begin by taking several deep breaths. Inhale the peace of God and exhale all stress, striving, and self-effort. Thank Jesus for His indwelling presence and filling. Listen to the Lord as you sit in His presence.

Connect

Jesus is the true temple and dwells inside of you. Sit with Jesus and meditate on His life inside you. Turn inward to your spirit and set your gaze on Him as you enjoy His presence.

Notes:

Day 22

God's Transforming Presence in Us

FROM THE HEAD...
Read: 1 Corinthians 3:16–17; 2 Corinthians 3:18

Study

In 1 Cor 3:16–17 we find another shift in the New Testament's use of temple language from the Old Testament. The word 'temple' here in 1 Cor 3 is not just a convenient or decorative metaphor but has its roots in the Old Testament accounts of the temple. As you recall, the Gospels showed the temple was fulfilled in and applied to Jesus. He is the true temple of God. In 1 Cor 3:16–17, we find God's people are the temple; those who follow Jesus become the temple of God as well. God's presence now dwells in His people, so they fulfill God's intention to dwell with humanity. The sequence seems to be that, first, Jesus Himself is the true temple of God, the place where God's presence dwells (since He is God), then, second, those who belong to Jesus and are in Christ by extension are also the temple where God dwells. What is true of Jesus becomes true of those who believe and belong to Him, since Jesus, the true temple, dwells in us. The blessings of God's presence get passed down from Jesus to us! Therefore, we are carriers of God's presence into the world.

God's Transforming Presence in Us

There are a couple of things to highlight in this passage that you read. When we read this passage we may be tempted to interpret this individualistically. I am a temple of God; my body is God's temple and He dwells within me personally. This is no doubt correct. But while true, there is far more to it than this. The pronouns are plural, "you all" (may be the best way to bring this out in English), and also the verb "'you all' are". Not only does it refer to individual Christians, but the church as a whole, which makes up the true temple, God's dwelling place. God is with us corporately. So, why does Paul bring up the church as God's temple where His presence resides? The verses right before it provide the key. In verses 1-15 the author addresses the issue of divisions within the church. The church in Corinth was divided over church leaders; they were split on whom to follow. This created division and endangered the destruction of the church. They are treating the church of Christ with disrespect by focusing on their favorite leaders—Paul, Apollos.

The one church in Corinth that Jesus himself created was now in danger of being divided by petty divisions among its members who insisted on giving their loyalty to favorite leaders. Now Paul reminds us the church is a holy temple where God's presence dwells. How dare we destroy it through creating divisions and factions within the church. It is holy and precious. It is sacred space. It is a sign of human reasoning and wisdom when we bring division into the church. As a temple, the church is God's holy possession, the place He chose to fill with His presence. We cannot take that lightly. That should affect how we view the church, and how we view others within the church. It is a serious matter to treat God's temple with disdain or disrespect. Instead, God calls His people to maintain its purity, health, and unity at all costs. This is the dwelling place of Almighty God.

It is encountering God's presence that produces holiness in His people. 2 Corinthians 3:18 tells us that when we gaze upon and contemplate the glory of the Lord, His presence, the result is being increasingly transformed into the image of Jesus. The way we become more like Jesus is by turning our gaze exclusively to Him. We share in that glory by being conformed to the image of the glorious One. It is the Holy Spirit that enables us to enter into a greater experience of the Lord's presence and experience His transforming power. Holiness does not begin with a list of rules and regulations, or a gritty determination to live a life of obedience. It begins by encountering God's presence; and when we do, we cannot help but be transformed into His likeness. Encountering God's glory will also keep us from giving our allegiance and worship to things that do not deserve it.

...TO THE HEART
Meditate

Read these verses out loud and emphasize different words while reading. "Don't you realize you are the temple of God? Don't you realize the spirit of the living God lives inside you?" Now, read again in the first person ("I am" ... "me"). Based on these verses, what does this mean practically in your relationship with family, and other believers? How does this change your perspective and responses with regards to cultivating unity?

Pray

Ask Holy Spirit to expose patterns of thought contrary to belonging to God and His church. Ask Holy Spirit to reveal mindsets that produce or entertain accusations, competition, superiority, selfish ambition, or any other fleshy response towards another. Write it down. Now ask Him to show you what He thinks of these individuals or people group. Write it down.

Connect

2 Corinthians 3:18 details how to embrace our glorious new reality as the bride of Christ and be totally transformed into heaven's reality, living from the inner chamber by being transformed through

what we behold! Take the areas you wrote down from above and lay each of these at the feet of Jesus. Allow the King of Glory to meet you in the deepest place in your soul. Commit to hiding yourself under the shadow of His wings when these mindsets intrude, and worship Him when you begin to feel that offense rise up. Speak out loud the Holy Spirit's perspective over your soul and these individuals. May you be filled to overflowing with His love and power working IN you to bring forth His nature through you. His aim and desire is for your highest satisfaction, to live with overwhelming joy and explosion of fullness of His presence that fills and satisfies every longing.

Notes:

Day 23

Building Blocks in God's Temple

FROM THE HEAD...

Read: Ephesians 2:20-22

Study

Since God is unchanging, God's presence has not changed. Since creation, God has not deviated one centimeter from His intention to establish His presence with man. What changed is the *way* He has shown His presence throughout history: First through a physical building, the tabernacle and temple; then through a single person, Jesus Christ; and now through Holy Spirit to His people, the church. The other changeable is whom God manifested His presence to. In the Old Testament it was primarily the nation of Israel. They were His covenant people, the tabernacle and temple was in their midst. What change has now taken place! In Christ, all people, Jews and Gentiles, make up the true people of God and His temple where His presence resides. In Eph 2:20-22 Paul describes a temple, a dwelling of God with foundations and building blocks. It is a temple that is still being built on its foundation. However, this is not a physical building, like the Old Testament temple structure made of stones and wood. It now consists of God's *people themselves*, with Jesus as the chief cornerstone.

Verses 11–19 describes two separate people groups, Jews and Gentiles, that were at enmity with each other before Christ's coming. Gentiles were seen as outsiders to the covenant people of God; they were unclean, with no hope to share in God's promises. Now, because of Jesus, one new humanity has been created, consisting of Jews and Gentiles as equal members. They are now one people, not two, and constitute one family. They now have equal *access* (v. 18). What do they have access to? God's presence! *Access* is temple language! Having access to God's presence was previously restricted primarily to the temple and Israel in the Old Testament, even more specifically to the priests. The reason we can all equally encounter God now is because *we are* the holy temple of God, the place where His presence resides through His Spirit (vv. 20–22). The physical temple was only a symbol of the greater presence of God with His people through His Spirit.

This temple also has foundations, which consist of the apostles and prophets, the leaders of the church. The individual members make up the building blocks contributing to the building of this holy temple. In Eph 2, the temple reminds us there is unity with the body of Christ. There is one people, consisting of all races and ethnicities. The church is a place where all people, despite ethnicity and status, encounter God. Paul intends the readers of this passage to not only accept each other as equal members of this new community, the temple, but they should also respond in extreme humility and gratitude for what God has done. It is a privilege to not only belong to, but to make up, God's temple. We have access to God through this temple and it is not to be taken lightly. Furthermore, being part of God's temple creates a new sense of belonging and identity. The church is not just a gathering of people on Sundays. We are the carriers of the very presence of God. We are the place where God chooses to manifest His presence, and where we encounter Him in worship. What a humbling and remarkable truth!

...TO THE HEART

Meditate

Paul specifically closes Eph 2 by emphasizing unity. Christ is our peace that reconciles and puts to death enmity, even within the church. Everyone is brought together as one in Christ. Communion is one act which signifies identifying with Jesus' blood and proclaiming His forgiveness over ourselves and others. It is through and by Jesus' blood we are empowered to forgive and walk in love and unity. It was also at the very first communion, the Lord's supper, the worst historical betrayal occurred in Jesus' life. Judas, Jesus' close friend and disciple, shared communion right before betraying Him, which led to His death. Even in the presence of our enemies the Lord has prepared a table before us, that table being the Lord's body. Through the table, by identifying with His death and resurrection, we are able to forgive what the world deems unforgivable and extend blessing towards those who have hurt us. We are able to partake of His body in the presence of betrayers and offenders which ultimately empowers us to extend not only forgiveness, but blessing and love. Cultivate this mindset and expectation before beginning the exercise of communion for today's devotional.

Pray

Before you begin, prepare the elements for communion. As you take the elements, verbally forgive by name those that come to mind. Release Jesus' love over them, bless them out loud by name. Imagine coming to the Lord's table with them. Open your heart to allow the love of Christ to pour in liquid love.

Connect

Speak over your heart, "I am the dwelling place of God. God lives in me, and I live in Him. Jesus lives in me, and I live in Him. I am washed by His blood and empowered by Him to love and walk just as He did." Imagine the capacity of your heart growing.

Notes:

Day 24

He Will Give You Rest

FROM THE HEAD...

Read: Hebrews 3:7–4:11

Study

One of the key themes found in the book of Hebrews is the superiority of Jesus Christ to anything found in the Old Covenant: Jesus is superior to the angels; He is superior to Moses; He is superior to the sacrificial system, and He offers up a superior sacrifice (Himself); and now He serves in a superior tabernacle (a heavenly one). In Heb 3–4 Jesus offers a superior rest to that offered in the Old Testament to the Israelites. In the Old Testament, those under Moses did not enter the promised land or experience rest because of rebellion and unbelief. As discipline, God made them wander in the wilderness for forty years until He raised up a new generation of Israelites who would enter the land. He also raised up a new leader, Joshua. Joshua eventually led the Israelites into the promised land, and it was here they would experience God's presence and rest. However, the author of Hebrews makes it clear in Heb 3–4 that the rest Joshua gave them was not the final rest God intended for His people. The rest that Israel experienced only pointed to a greater rest we now have access to and can experience in Jesus Christ. Therefore, the offer of entering God's rest still stands. There is a rest still available for God's people to enter into: "Therefore, since the promise of entering his rest still stands. . . ." (4:1). And now it is Jesus our high priest who leads us into this rest.

These verses are more than just a statement that rest is available. They are more than just a theological reflection on what rest is. They are an urgent warning for us not to miss this rest, like the first generation of Israelites did: "Therefore, since the promise of entering his rest still stands, let us be careful that none of you be found to have fallen short of it" (4:1). Instead, we are commanded to strive to enter the rest: "Let us therefore make every effort [strive] to enter that rest" (4:11). That is a disturbing prospect: It is possible to miss this rest! It is possible to commit the same mistake as the Israelites when they couldn't enter their rest because of rebellion and unbelief. God commands us not to miss this rest that still lies before us because of unbelief. Again, entering God's rest is not just an added bonus to the Christian life, but a command. We can miss out if we are not vigilant.

So what is this rest that Jesus provides which the author of Hebrews refers to? For the people of Israel it was entering the earthly, physical promised land, the place where God manifested his presence among His people. However, this only foreshadowed a greater rest still to come now available through Jesus. Entering into God's rest in Christ is probably another way of saying what we find in 10:19: *Entering* into the most Holy Place through the blood of Christ. The very next verse after the offer of rest in 4:1–13 commands us to approach God's throne. In Heb 4:14–16 the author tells us that since we have such a great High Priest in Jesus, "Let us then approach God's throne of grace with confidence, so that we may receive mercy and find grace to help us in our time of need." Jesus does something that no priest in the Old Testament could do: Lead people right into the very throne room of God, into a direct encounter with God. It is here we find all the resources necessary to live as God's people.

Putting this all together, entering Christ's rest is nothing less than entering into God's manifest presence, and resting in Him.

The idea of "rest" signifies ceasing from own striving and efforts, resting and trusting in the Lord, standing in stillness before Him. To experience the rest that Jesus gives is to encounter the presence of God through faith and prayer. It is Jesus Himself who leads us into rest. Doubt and unbelief block us from experiencing rest in God's presence. However, it is faith that lays hold of the promise of entering His rest and experiencing the glorious presence of God. Don't miss that rest!

...TO THE HEART
Meditate

Why did it take the Israelites 40 years to go on an 11-day journey to the Promised Land? What was God's perspective on this from Heb 3–4? Was the issue a lack of presence? Did the Israelites have God's presence previously? Even though they saw God's works, they did not know His ways. What does this mean? How can you see and experience God's works and presence but not know His ways in your own life? Look up the Greek word "know" used in this verse. Does this word for "know" signify something other than mere intellectual knowledge?

The Israelites exchanged an experiential knowing and trusting of God for doubt and unbelief, treating God's word and presence with contempt. Instead of reminding themselves who their God is, they doubted His character and questioned His nature towards them. When it feels like God is no longer acting on our behalf, the warning is to hold steadfastly to the beginning of our confidence, returning to our first love in 'knowing' Him (see Rev 2:4–5). This is when we actually become partakers of Christ, entering into His rest, the peace that surpasses all understanding, when we continue steadfastly on with active faith. This active experiential 'knowing' is also directly connected with entering His rest. This is accomplished by turning our gaze towards Jesus.

Pray

Identify areas of unbelief or doubt of God's goodness, provision, or care for you and your future. Ask Jesus to bring to mind any instances you felt abandoned by God, disappointed by life circumstances or hope deferred. Once identified, ask Him to reveal any lies about God or beliefs you formed in response to the pain you experienced during your own wilderness time. Confess these to the Lord and exchange these beliefs with truths. Recommit yourself and every area of your life to your Father. Speak your commitment to trust Him in the areas you don't see or feel His goodness. Ask Him to help your unbelief with difficult areas.

Connect

If you are currently in, or came out of, a trial season and find doubt and unbelief more familiar than a childlike trust, spend a few moments recalling what God has done for you in your past and write this down. Next, write down what you have experienced of His character. Lastly, turn your gaze on Jesus and worship Him, with an abandoned heart of complete surrender and childlike trust.

Thirty Days in God's Presence

Notes:

Day 25

Drawing Near to God through Our High Priest

FROM THE HEAD...

Read: Hebrews 9:6–14; 10:19–25

Study

The book of Hebrews contrasts two ways God's presence is made known and experienced. First, under the Old Covenant, God's presence was revealed in the physical tabernacle and temple through the Old Covenant priesthood of Aaron. This meant offering up sacrifices and atoning for the sins of the people in the earthly tabernacle and temple. Secondly, under the new system or New Covenant, the way to God's presence has now been revealed in and through Christ. It is through the One who is the radiance of God's glory (Heb 1:3), that we are led into the very presence of God in heaven. The earthly tabernacle, while it mediated God's presence to His people Israel, served just as much to restrict God's presence as to make it available. The tabernacle (and temple) had an outer court, an inner court or Holy place, and the most Holy place. The Most Holy Place, or Holy of Holies, which contained the ark of the covenant and where God's presence rested, was separated from the rest of the building by a curtain. Only one person, Israel's high priest, could enter it—and then only once a year on the Day of Atonement. The full experience of God's presence was guarded, restricted to the high priest, and limited to one day a year.

How different for us now under Christ Jesus! He has paved the way for us to enter the true heavenly dwelling of God, of which the earthly temple in Israel was only a shadow or reflection. Hebrews 9 states that Jesus himself has entered the true, heavenly tabernacle, offered up the final, once-for-all sacrifice of Himself in order to remove sin that was a barrier to the full enjoyment of God's presence.

In Heb 10:19-25, we find the author's application of these truths from chapter 9. If Christ is our high priest and opened the way into the heavenly tabernacle, then we must avail ourselves of that reality. Since Jesus offered up the final, eternal sacrifice for our sins, we have immediate and unhindered access to His heavenly throne room and the Holy of Holies. The urgent call to approach God's presence back in 4:14-16 is now repeated in 10:19-25: "Let us draw near to God with a sincere heart in full assurance." Notice this is not a recommendation, or an option only when we need it; it is a command: "Let us draw near to God." In Greek "Let us draw near" is called a *hortatory* construction. The term 'hortatory' means to urge and exhort. We are being urged and commanded to approach God's throne, to avail ourselves of God's presence. Because of the work of Christ, our High Priest, on the cross to atone for sin, we now have complete confidence to enter the Holy of Holies. This is something that could not be done in the Old Testament. We have direct and unlimited access because of our High Priest, Jesus. He cleanses us, so we can enter with boldness. We have confidence to not just enter in, but to draw *near* to God. We can have the most intimate encounter - anyone, at any time. It would be senseless not to take full advantage of this.

There was also a curtain separating the Holy of Holies from the rest of the tabernacle and temple. Verse 20 tells us that Jesus' body which He gave up for us as a sacrifice is the curtain. The curtain in the temple brought separation; it closed off the Holy of

Holies. However, now Jesus is the curtain which means access is no longer closed off. Rather, His body is the means of access into God's presence for all who approach Him in faith. It is as if we enter the temple, only to find no curtain restricting the Holy of Holies. Since the coming of Christ to offer Himself as a sacrifice as our High Priest, we can now do something that no one has been able to do since the Garden of Eden: We (not just the priest) can go directly into God's presence, we can approach God and draw near to Him at any time (not just once a year). So, how do we respond? Do not miss out on this amazing blessing. Let us draw near to God in full assurance!

. . .TO THE HEART
Meditate

One can gauge God's value for the secret place of His presence by considering this compelling urgent command given in Heb 10. The innermost chamber of the temple, the Holy of Holies, was the closest one could come before God, and only reserved for the high priest to enter on your behalf. Just as the marriage bed is intended for only two, representing the most sacred intimacy between husband and wife, so the Holy of Holies is reserved for intimate connection between God and His people. Our God is a jealous God, longing for intimacy with us. There is a place for corporate worship and prayer. However, there is a reason He places priority on our intimacy with Him first. What does this look like in your own life? What does the word "boldly" mean in Heb 4:16? If you lack boldness or confidence in approaching Him, what is hindering you? What is a sin consciousness? How does it differ from a consciousness of righteousness? Does this ever affect your boldness in coming before the Lord?

Pray

Go into a private place where you will be undistracted. Read the declarations from Heb 10 over yourself slowly. Engage your spirit and mind into stepping through the outer courts, the inner courts, and entering into the holy of holies through these truths. Wrap your heart tightly around these truths, knowing you are encountering the King of Glory! If it is difficult to engage your heart, remember something that God has done for you personally and thank Him for that, or begin singing out loud to Him. Press in with boldness. Run into His arms and continue engaging your spirit.

Connect

If Jesus made the way and God has extended the invitation, the only hindrance is ourselves. We must hold tightly, without wavering to the hope we say we have. We must respond in belief to this fundamental truth, anchoring ourselves in His reality regardless of how we feel. Speaking God's truth over ourselves changes our molecular structure. Our thoughts are transformed, emotions align with His truth, and our heart comes alive. Read through Heb 10 and write down truths for you personally to declare over yourself. For example:

> "I am made holy by the sacrifice of the body of Jesus, I am cleansed from sin and cleansed from a sin consciousness. Jesus is my High Priest who is forever making me holy. I am in covenant with the Lord who has put His law in my heart. I can come confidently and boldly into heaven's most holy place right now because of Jesus' blood. I trust fully and completely in God and know that I am made clean. Not only does God ask me to come to Him regularly and boldly, He is eagerly waiting for me!"

Notes:

Day 26

Priests Who Worship in His Temple

FROM THE HEAD...
Read: 1 Peter 2:4–10
Study

By now you are beginning to see the theme of God's presence all over the Scriptures, in both Old and New Testaments. You could say it is the thread that ties the entire Bible together. The "presence of God" is woven through every single book in some way. Another important passage for understanding God's presence is the book of 1 Peter. We encounter both temple and priestly language in 1 Pet 2:4–10. Chapter 2 begins with a building constructed of living stones. This is not a literal, physical building, but metaphorically refers to the church as in the people of God. It is called a "spiritual house" in verse 5 with Christ as the main cornerstone of this building. He is the precious cornerstone, the most important foundational part of the building that holds the whole spiritual structure together. Everything must be built on Jesus. Though the word "temple" is not used here, the spiritual house is clearly meant to be a temple. The people of God, the living stones, make up this spiritual temple which is where God's presence dwells. This is similar to what we saw in Eph 2:20-22: The church is being built up into a holy temple where God's presence dwells through His Spirit.

In 1 Pet 2, the temple is currently under construction, as those who come to Christ in faith are added to the building to become a holy dwelling place of God's presence. However, in this spiritual temple the people are also priests that serve. That's right, they are both the temple and the priests at the same time! Right after saying they are a spiritual house he calls the people a holy priesthood. Later in verses 9-10 they are called a "royal priesthood". These words were applied first to Israel in the Old Testament (Exod 19:6); but now are applied to the church, the people of God, whether Jews or Gentiles. As we saw in the Old Testament, priests were necessary to mediate the presence of God to the people. They represented the people before God, served Him, and offered up sacrifices. But the role of the priest did not end with the coming of Jesus and the New Covenant. Now all of God's people, not just those in the line of Aaron, serve as God's priests who have unique access to God's presence in the spiritual temple, the church. They are mediators of God's presence to the world.

Priests in the Old Testament were to be holy in order to serve in the temple. Now, God's new priests, those that make up the church, are to be holy as God himself is holy (1 Pet 1:15). Priests in the Old Testament offered up sacrifices of animals for their own sins, and for the sins of the people. Now this new priesthood offers up spiritual sacrifices that are acceptable to God. The sacrifices they offer are themselves (see Rom 12:1), and of praise and worship. In 1 Pet 2:9 we are to declare the praises of God, as priests, to worship Him. These verses describe the church's vocation, their destiny, and their true identity. In a corrupt and hostile world, the vocation and identity of the people of God is that of a holy temple who host God's very presence. They are priests who have the honor of mediating God's presence to the world while offering up spiritual sacrifices of praise and worship. This is who the people of God are. What an honor and privilege!

...TO THE HEART
Meditate

You. You have been chosen and anointed to serve as a priest before God, the infinite and holy One, the Alpha and Omega. He is glorious and majestic, the Sovereign Creator and King of Kings. What a glorious honor! What was the function of priests in this passage? The role of ministering TO the Lord was described as one who waited on, served, or attended to God. See Deut 10:8; 18:5. How is being a part of a kingdom of priests significant for you today? Ps 135 tells us to, "Praise the Lord, all you servants of the Lord who *minister* in the house of the Lord in the courts of the house of our God." The praise you personally bring Him ministers to His heart. Your pain and your joys elicit a response that can only come from the testimony He has written in your heart. Bringing this before the Lord is serving Him as a priest, and actually affects a response from Him as you minister to Him. When fully understood, this should result in the most outrageous response of praise and adoration in blessing the Lord! Another role of priest was to mediate God's presence to the world. In what way can you mediate, or represent, God and carry His presence to the world?

Pray

Begin by thanking Jesus for His specific attributes and focusing your heart on Jesus' love for you. Speak aloud your love and affection for Him. Allow your heart to come alive in His love and adoration of His character

Connect

Spend 10 minutes, three times a day for the next five days in adoring worship, ministering to God's heart. A few ideas for these 10-minute soaking sessions are below. Follow Holy Spirit and His prompting for your heart in that moment.

Priests Who Worship in His Temple

1. Sing a song from your heart to Him.
2. Listen to worship music that extols God's name and nature, sing to Him out loud.
3. Pick someplace you go everyday, whether it be your car, the restroom, walking the dog, etc.. and set aside consistent time to worship. Kneel, lift your hands, or sing out loud to the Lord. Do something that catapults your body into a space of adoration and worship.

Notes:

Day 27

Living in the Light of God's Presence

FROM THE HEAD...

Read: 1 John 1:5–7

Study

Light and darkness; they are complete opposites. They cannot occupy the same space. When light shines, it overcomes darkness. In 1 John, light stands for God's presence, but also goodness, truth, purity, and absolute holiness of God's character. Because God is light, there is no darkness in Him at all (v. 5). Darkness refers to that which is evil, false, and impure. It is the absence of God's presence. Therefore, since God is light, darkness cannot exist in Him. Based on this, light and darkness also refer to two life styles: To live in the light is to live in God's presence and reflect His holy character. To live in the light is to live in the truth. To live in the darkness is to live a life of impurity, falsehood, and deceit. To live in darkness is a failure to live in God's presence and reflect His character.

Light and darkness are concepts from the Old Testament. Light referred to God's presence, His pure and holy character.

When the Israelites traveled through the desert on their way to the promised land, a pillar of fire gave them light at night to guide their way. In the tabernacle and temple was a golden lampstand that illuminated the Holy Place, representing the presence of God. The prophets use the language of light to refer to God's presence with His people. Isaiah 60:1 prophesies a coming day when the light will shine once more in Jerusalem. The second line of the verse says "and the glory of the Lord rises upon you." The light to come and shine is the very glory of God. That is, God's presence would rise and shine over His people. Prior to this, thick darkness was over the people, (v. 2) as they were in sin, without illumination or hope. However, the brilliant light of God's glory that previously filled the tabernacle and temple will now return to the people, who were exiled because of sin. They will encounter God's glory and presence once again.

This concept of light and darkness is the backdrop for understanding light and darkness in 1 John 1:5-7. To live in the light is to live in God's presence, and therefore to reflect his character. To live in the darkness is to live in sin, resulting in gloom and hopelessness outside of God's presence. However, we cannot resolve to live a life of holiness on our own as 1 John states. Walking in the light only comes from abiding in the very presence of God, who is light. If God is light - holy and pure - then it follows that those who live in His presence will indeed reflect His holiness. When one spends time in the light of God's presence, darkness can no longer exist and it can no longer characterize us. To think we can live in the light of God's presence, while at the same time in the darkness of sin, is to live a deceptive lie (v. 6). We are either in the light or in darkness. As we walk in God's presence, we will walk also in the light.

...TO THE HEART
Meditate

Think about the dynamic between light and darkness. How does one walk in the light? What does this practically look like on a daily basis for you? Exodus 33:18-20 gives us an example of what to expect with the story of Moses on Mt Sinai.

"Then Moses said, 'Now, please show me your glory (his manifest presence)" The Lord answered, "I will cause all my goodness to pass in front of you, and I will announce my name, the Lord, so you can hear it... When Moses came down from Mt Sinai with the two tablets of the covenant law in his hands, he was not aware that his face was radiant because he had spoken with the Lord." What happened to Moses face when he came down from being in God's presence? Moses was required to veil his face because his countenance was so bright - it blinded! What is more astounding than this historical fact lies in 2 Cor 3. We are told that Moses' experience was under the old covenant and how much *more so* should our faces shine when we mirror Christ as we gaze upon Him. "Even the ministry that was characterized by chiseled letters on stone tablets came with a dazzling measure of glory, though it produced death. The Israelites couldn't bear to look on the glowing face of Moses because the radiant splendor shining from his countenance- a glory destined to fade away, as it was under the old testament law code. Yet how much MORE radiant is this new and glorious ministry of the Spirit that shines in us!" (2 Cor 3:7-18).

We have access to an increasingly greater glory than that of even Moses. We have the very same Spirit living in us that Moses encountered on the mountain and is described in the New Testament. This can and should be our experience as well in even greater measure. Are you convinced that He who raised Jesus from the dead lives inside you? Are you convinced that you can come boldly before Him and mirror His glory as you are transformed into His likeness? If so, what should your expectation be when you come boldly before the Lord?

Pray

Find a quiet place to sit. Turn your affection and gaze to Jesus. Wait on the Lord. Sing to Him if your mind begins to wander. Wait until your spirit is engaged. Slowly meditate on the verses below, one verse at a time. Read out loud in first person and pray this passage to the Lord, as the cry of your heart.

> "But whenever anyone turns to the Lord from his sins, then the veil is taken away. 17 The Lord is the Spirit who gives them life, and where he is there is freedom from trying to be saved by keeping the laws of God. 18 But we Christians have no veil over our faces; we can be mirrors that brightly reflect the glory of the Lord. And as the Spirit of the Lord works within us, we become more and more like him" (2 Cor 3:14-18)

Connect

Write down your expectations when you come before God's Presence this week in your secret place. What are you expecting? Re-read and meditate on 1 Cor 3:14-18 in your time with Jesus.

Notes:

Day 28

A Heavenly Worship Service

FROM THE HEAD...

Read: Revelation 4:1–11

Study

Did you know the book of Revelation is primarily a book about worship? That's right. We often associate Revelation with endtimes predictions of the future. But the book's true concern is worship. Revelation answers the question: Who is truly worthy of our worship and allegiance? Who is deserving of our devotion and affections? Is it Caesar, Rome, some other human ruler, or is it God and the Lamb alone? You cannot serve two masters. Scan through Revelation and notice how many hymns and songs are sung by groups and individuals. In Rev 4–5 John's vision begins with a stirring scene of worship in the heavenly throne room. We get to listen into someone else's worship service! What John sees is the heavenly temple, the throne room, where God dwells. It is the same temple Isaiah entered (Isa 6:1–8), and the same temple Ezekiel was privileged to glimpse (Ezek 1–2). Now John is a witness to a celestial worship service in the very presence of God, His Holy of Holies! At the center of heaven is God's throne. God's throne is a

A Heavenly Worship Service

symbol of His sovereignty and authority, with all of heaven gathering around and rendering Him ceaseless worship.

Notice how God is described in chapter 4. One gets the impression that John, the author, is trying to describe what cannot easily be described! God's appearance is as jasper and ruby, with a rainbow-like emerald surrounding Him. These precious jewels portray beauty and purity of the glorious presence of God. The author does not describe God in detail (His shape, face, body, arms, legs), like he does the Son of Man in chapter 1. Rather, John is overwhelmed with His appearance and glorious presence. The scene is beautiful, brilliant, and breathtaking! Everything begins with God's presence and extends out from there. John describes the appearance of the One on the throne, then moves to the environs around it. Encircling the throne are twenty-four other thrones with elders seated on them. The elders are probably angelic beings who attend to worshiping God. They may be heavenly representatives of God's people on earth. Lightning and thunder emanate from the throne, displaying God's holiness and justice. He is to be approached with reverence and awe. The seven Spirits are also before the throne - this is probably a metaphorical way of referring to the Holy Spirit, and recalls the seven spirits in Isa 11:2. There is also a smooth sea before the throne. It is like glass, suggesting calmness, control, serenity. Lastly, there are four living creatures, angelic beings that represent all creation. Like the twenty-four elders, their main job is to render worship, probably anticipating the worship that all creation (four is the number of the world and of creation) would one day render God (and the Lamb) on the throne in Rev 22:3. Heaven is a place of order, beauty, serenity, and awe, as this is the dwelling place of God. God sits enthroned at the center of all reality. The angelic beings respond with unceasing praise and worship.

"Holy, Holy, Holy is the Lord God Almighty, who was and is and is to come."

"You are worthy, our Lord and God, to receive glory and honor and power, for you created all things, and by your will they were created and have their being."

All heaven worships and adores God in His temple because He is Holy, set apart and far above creation. God is the creator of all that exists. He is worshiped because He is the sovereign ruler over all. In other words, heaven worships God simply for who He is! This is why we, His people, should worship Him here on earth! When God's people worship, they are reflecting, but also joining in with the endless praise in heaven. When we worship today, we join the angels acknowledging who God is in His very presence.

...TO THE HEART
Meditate

In the Lord's prayer, we pray "Our Father who is in heaven, holy is your name. Your kingdom come, your will be done on earth as it is in heaven." This passage from Rev 4 is a glimpse into what we are asking for when we pray the Lord's prayer. When we ask for God's will to be done on earth as it is in heaven, we are asking for the demonstration of Rev 4 on earth. God's reality in heaven can be realized on earth, or else Jesus would not have instructed us to specifically pray for this. After reading Rev 4, what is one of the ways we can manifest heaven's realities on earth? What was the response of the heavenly beings, and what was their posture?

Pray

Sit in a silent place, uninterrupted. Meditate on Rev 4:1–11, word by word, line by line. Ask Holy Spirit to encounter you as you worship God. With this expectation, worship with the others in heaven "Holy, holy, holy, Lord God Almighty, who was and is and is to come. You are worthy, O Lord, to receive glory and honor and power; For You created all things, and by Your will they exist and were created." Humble yourself before the throne. Allow the worship of His majesty to overwhelm you and stay in this posture as you read and meditate.

A Heavenly Worship Service

Connect

Frances Metcalfe wrote of an encounter she had with the Lord that took her out of her body. She describes the encounter here: "Whatever the type of rapture, I have found that always, if it is complete, it takes me out of myself-out of my own mind and ways, and even out of my identity at times. I am not conscious of myself as an individual, but only as a part of this wonderful Body, "hidden away with Christ in God." Thus there is no sense of personal satisfaction or elation in the reception of these divine favors, we do not receive these things as unto ourselves. In fact, self does not enter at all into these celestial affairs. Oh, great is this deliverance from our worst enemy, even our own self! While here in the earth we must constantly watch and be on guard, lest SELF defraud God and assert prerogatives over our will. However, while in the state of complete rapture, self is temporarily inactive, and for a time we are lost in God. The longest sustained period of rapture I have experienced was during this eight days, and I lived in constant communion with the Lord in the Spirit."[1] As you come before the throne of God, expect the same type of abandoned worship spoken of in Revelation. These encounters with God will lead to seeing Him rightly by constantly declaring his holiness while losing sight of self and being consumed with His majesty.

---

1. Maloney, *Ladies of Gold Volume 2*, 25.

THIRTY DAYS IN GOD'S PRESENCE

Notes:

Day 29

Who Can Stand in God's Presence?

FROM THE HEAD...

Read: Revelation 7:9–17

Study

The book of Revelation gives us a real time glimpse into God's throne room, His heavenly Temple. The temple the Israelites constructed was only a visible reflection, merely a model, of the true heavenly temple where God's throne is. We already entered the heavenly temple back in Rev 4–5 through John's vision. Now we encounter God here again in Rev 7:9–17. What John sees is the same scene as in Rev 4–5. God's throne is at the center of the vision with the Lamb. All the angels, the elders, and the four living creatures surround the throne and worship.

But there is another group here that was not present in chapters 4–5. Now an innumerable multitude of saints, a multicultural group from every tribe, tongue, language, and nation, also stands before the throne. These are the people of God that are experiencing God's presence in His heavenly temple. When it seems that God's people are a powerless minority in the world, this vision shows our belonging to a great throng of people who are marked by worship in God's presence. The people of God are described as wearing white robes and holding palm branches. This signifies joyful celebration in the presence of God, perhaps the heavenly celebration of the Feast of Tabernacles. In response to being before Him, they cry out in song: "Salvation belongs to our God, who sits on the throne, and to the Lamb" (v. 10). The angels who are around the throne also respond by falling on their faces and worshiping: "Amen! Praise and glory and wisdom and thanksgiving and honor and power and strength be to our God for ever and ever. Amen!" (v. 12). It is one big heavenly worship service! This may be a glimpse into the future when God's people stand in His presence when Christ returns to bring His kingdom. However, we can experience this right now. Like the readers of the book of Hebrews, we can approach the throne of God, and enter into the very Holy of Holies in the heavenly temple. We don't have to wait until the future.

This innumerable multitude of God's people is further described as those who have washed their robes by the blood of Jesus (v. 14). In other words, while God requires purity and holiness of those who would approach His presence, it is ultimately the finished work of Christ on the cross that makes us worthy to enter into the presence of a holy God. The very next verse reiterates the main privilege we enjoy in God's presence: We serve God night and day in His temple, and in turn His presence shelters us. Serving God was the role of the priests in the Old Testament. Now as His priests we serve Him continually in His presence. What an incredible picture! God's people worshiping and serving in God's presence, and God's presence covering and sheltering them. This vision reminds us of our true identity and purpose: To serve God as His priests, in His presence. At the same time, it assures us that when God's people face a world of trouble, distress, pain, and turmoil we find protection in God's sheltering presence.

...TO THE HEART
Meditate

As this passage depicts, what is occurring right now in the heavenly temple? According to this passage, what is everyone doing that surrounds the throne? What would you define worship as? When we worship, we focus our attention on the true center of all reality, God seated on His throne. Worship is an act of divesting ourselves of our own interests, our own agendas, our pride, and focusing on the One who is sovereign over all things. Worship and rest in God's presence is actually the reward for living faithfully and sacrificially amidst earthly turmoil and trouble. The great multitude in chapter 7 has come through tribulation, and now they stand in God's presence. How can you practice your identity as a priest? What is a practical response when you encounter turmoil and pain?

Pray

Read Rev 7:9-17 slowly four times. Emphasize each song to God when you read out loud. Imagine what you are reading. Revelation was written in part so that you could 'reexperience' what John saw in his visions. You are part of a great multitude, a huge gathering before the throne of God in heaven. As you place yourself before His throne, reflect on what God has done for you in His Son, Jesus, the salvation He has provided, the sacrifice on the cross He has made, the righteousness and holiness He has given. Tell Him out loud the privilege and honor it is of encountering Him personally and respond in praise.

Connect

Worship orients our vision and perspective towards the One who is faithful and who is in control of all things, whose presence is a sheltering cover. Where do you feel overwhelmed, stressed or anxious? What do you face today that feels threatening and impossible? Write these down. Now, respond in worship to God. Picture

His presence as a shelter that protects you and continue to worship until His joy fills your heart.

Notes:

Day 30

Enjoying God's Presence Forever

FROM THE HEAD...
Read: Revelation 21:9–11; 22:1–5
Study

Now we finally come to the end! Both the end of the Bible, and the end of God's story to redeem humanity in order to restore His intention for us that was ruined by sin back in Gen 3. That intention was to establish His presence in creation in the midst of His people. We see the Bible has come full circle: God who dwelled with His people in his creation in Gen 1-2 is now dwelling with His people on a New Creation in Rev 21-22! Genesis 1-2 and Rev 21-22 form "bookends" around the entire Bible! In fact, notice all the parallels between Gen 1-2 and Rev 21-22.

Heavens and earth (Gen 1:1)	New Heavens and earth (Rev 21:1)
God walks with people in the Garden (Gen 3:8)	God is present with His people in the New Creation/Garden (Rev 21:3; 22:1-2)
River in the Garden (Gen 2:10)	River of life in the New Creation (Rev 22:1)

Enjoying God's Presence Forever

Tree of life in the Garden (Gen 2:9)	Tree of life in the New Creation (Rev 22:2)

You get the idea. The new creation of Rev 21–22 is the restored Garden of Eden, the place of God's presence with His people.

In fact, the glory of God, which once filled only the tabernacle and temple, now suffuses the entire city, New Jerusalem (Rev 21:11). God's intention in Genesis was to live with His people on earth. But sin barred enjoyment of God's presence, and Adam and Eve were removed from the Garden (Gen 3). Since God's intention was to live with His people, he had them construct a tabernacle, and then a temple, to mediate God's presence with His people. All of this was in anticipation of the day when God would once more live directly with His people on earth as He did in the Garden of Eden. And that is exactly what we find going on in Rev 21–22.

God's presence so suffuses the entire New Creation that there is no longer a need for a separate temple to house it! As he is describing what he saw, John mentions something he did not see: "And I did not see a temple in it, for God and the Lamb are its temple" (21:21). The presence of God and the Lamb with their people is what the temple pointed to all along. In fact, the entire city is one big temple, and its cube-shape in 21:16 even mirrors the shape of the Holy of Holies in the Old Testament temple: "Its length and width and height were equal" (see 1 Kgs 6:20). And both the Holy of Holies and the New Jerusalem are made of pure gold. Revelation 21–22 shows how all God's people now have immediate access to God's presence since sin and evil in this fallen world have been removed (Rev 20). These were the things that necessitated a physical temple in the first place. Now that sin and the old order of things are gone, God can dwell directly with His people as He did long ago in the garden. God's intention is that we enjoy full access to His presence. This is the most important thing about the final vision in Revelation: It is not about measurements, location, the appearance of the New Jerusalem, or what takes place there. What is central is that God and the Lamb are at the center of all things. All have equal and unhindered access to God's presence.

Revelation 4–5 shows God and the Lamb in heaven, with all heaven worshiping them in God's presence. What is true in heaven becomes a reality on earth. The throne of God and the Lamb in heaven are now found on a new earth. God is now fully present with His people, and they worship God in unending praise. Just as Jesus taught us to pray, "On earth as it is in heaven", Revelation is the answer to the prayer: On earth (Rev 21–22) as it is in heaven (Rev 4–5). Revelation is the story of how the heavenly vision of chapters 4–5 become a reality on earth in chapters 21–22. And so the Bible's story ends the way it began - with God dwelling with his people on earth, His people experiencing and enjoying His presence. This was God's intention from Gen 1–2, and this will be our portion forever. God created us for encounter with Him. Revelation 21–22 ends with us engaging in and pursuing what we were created for! If that is what we will be doing for eternity, we should be practicing and preparing for that right now!

...TO THE HEART
Meditate

In conclusion, what do you see God's original intention was in the Garden and in Revelation? How has God's presence with His people come full circle from Gen 1–2 to Rev 21–22? How would you summarize the main themes of God's presence in Scripture? What difference does, or should, this make in a believer's life?

Pray

Consider the last 30 days and allow your heart to recall and remember the ways the Lord has encountered you this past month. Let your heart soak in His presence and express your gratitude to Him. Engage your heart with His heart and sit with Him in this place.

Connect

Having experienced God's presence in the secret place, the call is to continue this one pursuit as your one desire. However, it shouldn't just be reserved for the secret place. As you encounter Him in secret, the aim is to abide in His presence throughout your day, your week, and your life. Live sacramentally. The secret place always has priority, and we live from that place as we go about our day. A.W Tozer addressed sacramental living the *Pursuit of God*: "Every act of...life is or can be truly as sacred as prayer or baptism or the Lord's supper. To say this is... to lift every act up into a living kingdom and turn the whole life into a sacrament."[1]

Blessings to you in the secret place as you encounter Him in your work, family and relationships. May you find and purchase the oil for your lamps and may you burn brighter with overflowing abundance from spending time in His presence.

---

1. Tozer, *The Pursuit of God*, 119–21.

Notes:

Works Cited

Maloney, James. *Ladies of Gold, Volume 2*. Bloomington: Westbow, 2015.
Tozer, A. W. *The Pursuit of God*. Chicago: Moody, 2015.

www.ingramcontent.com/pod-product-compliance
Lightning Source LLC
Chambersburg PA
CBHW071609170426
43196CB00034B/2252